THE ROTUNDA IN THESSALONIKI AND ITS MOSAICS

FIRST EDITION 2017
FIRST REPRINT FEBRUARY 2024

Cover Illustration: Portrait of the soldier martyr Onesiphoros (fig. 29).

ISBN 978-618-5209-11-7

KAPON EDITIONS
23–27 Makriyanni Str., Athens 117 42, Greece
Tel. (+30) 210 9235 098, (+30) 210 9214 089

RACHEL'S BOOKSHOP
22 Ploutarchou Str., Athens 106 76, Greece
Tel. (+30) 210 7241 442, (+30) 210 9210 983

www.kaponeditions.gr • linktr.ee/kapon_editions • info@kaponeditions.gr

BENTE KIILERICH – HJALMAR TORP

THE ROTUNDA IN THESSALONIKI AND ITS MOSAICS

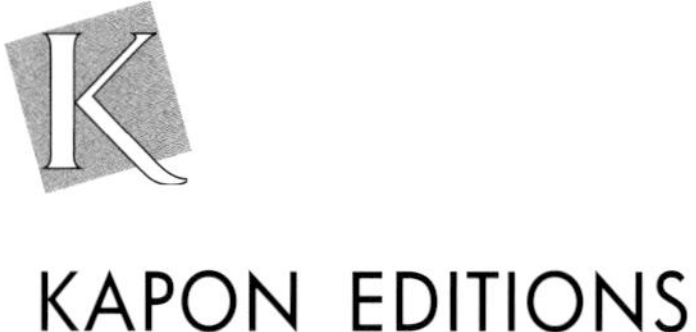

KAPON EDITIONS

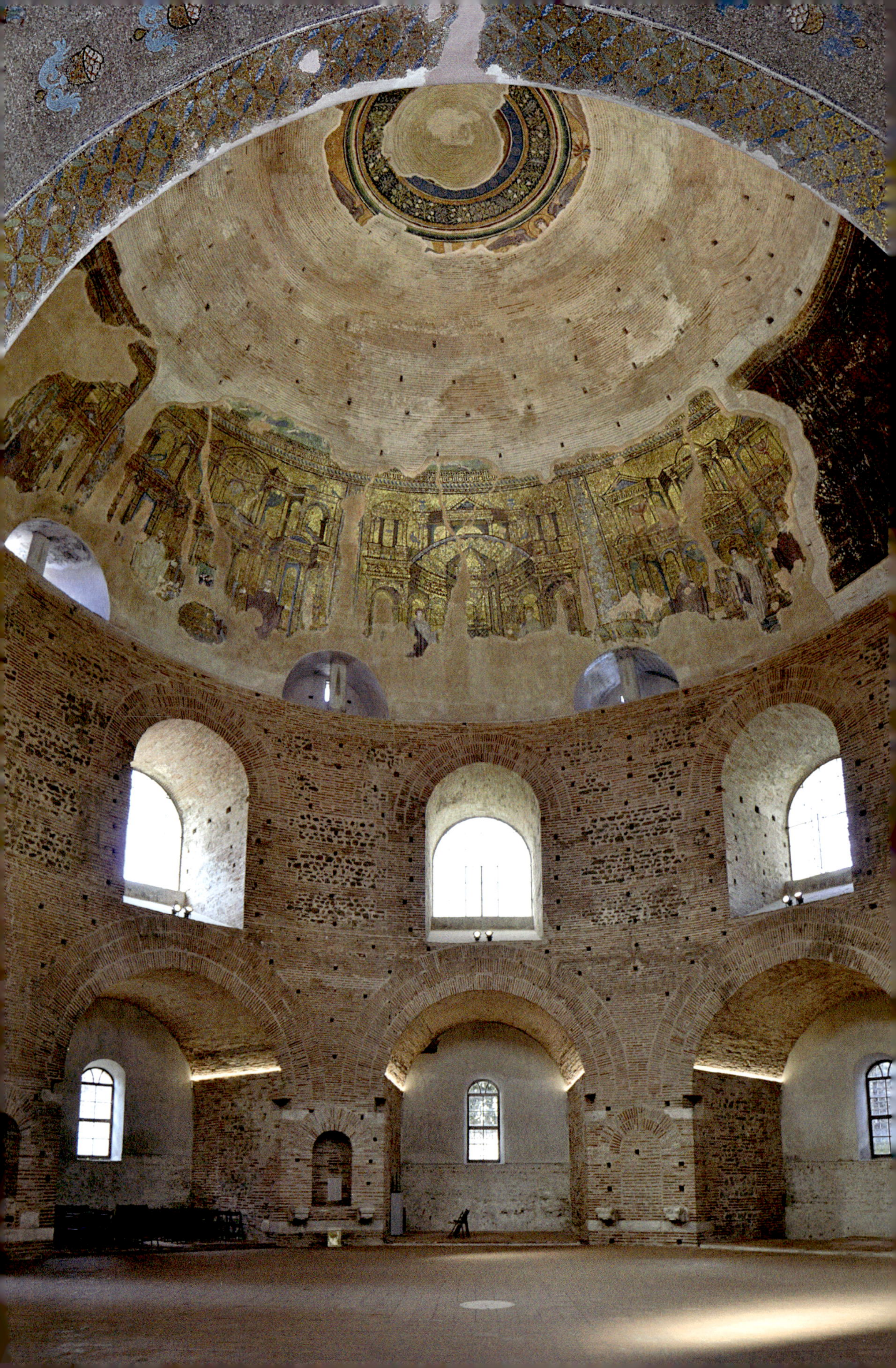

TABLE OF CONTENTS

Introduction

The mosaics in the Rotunda at Thessaloniki are by far the most exquisite mosaics preserved from the late antique and early Byzantine periods, not only in Thessaloniki, but in the late Roman world at large. After the earthquake in 1978, which seriously damaged the building and its decoration, scaffolds were set up in view of the impeding restauration. For decades these structures covered large parts of the interior walls and most of the mosaics. From the floor one could see the cupola medallion and the upper part of the architectural zone, but the martyrs inhabiting this architectural scenery were almost totally hidden. When the scaffolding was removed in December 2015, the martyrs and the architectural zone appeared again in full panoramic view. This new situation allows a complete overview of the extant mosaics. After a visit to Thessaloniki around New Year 2015/2016, it inspired us to write this book about the Rotunda and its magnificent mosaic decoration.

This small book is intended as an introduction to the Rotunda, as a guide when visiting the building and as a summary and update of the present state of research on the monument. Within its limited format, it is impossible for us to discuss all aspects of the architecture and the mosaics. A bibliography lists recent books and articles on various aspects of the monument and in particular the mosaics. In these works one can find detailed discussions of the mosaics, ranging from the problems of chronology to questions of style and iconography. For a presentation of the mosaics in combination with the other Byzantine monuments in Thessaloniki, we refer readers to the large and fully illustrated Kapon publication by Charalambos Bakirtzis, Eftychia Kourkoutidou-Nikolaïdou and Chrysanthi Mavropoulou-Tsioumi, *Mosaics of Thessaloniki, 4th-14th Century* (2012), in Greek and English editions. More specific points are discussed in the forthcoming companion volume *The Mo-*

1. Interior view of Rotunda in December 2015 after the removal of the scaffolds.

2. Longitudinal cross-section (E-W) of the Rotunda, showing the mosaics (drawing by W.S. George, 1907).

saics of Thessaloniki Revisited,* Papers from the workshop at the Courtauld Institute of Art, University of London, 30 May 2014 (in press), edited by Antony Eastmond and Myrto Hatzaki; this work contains three contributions dealing explicitly with the Rotunda. We hope the present book and its illustrations will stimulate interest in this unique monument and in Byzantine art, archaeology and aesthetics in general.

BENTE KIILERICH and HJALMAR TORP
Bergen, April 2016

2

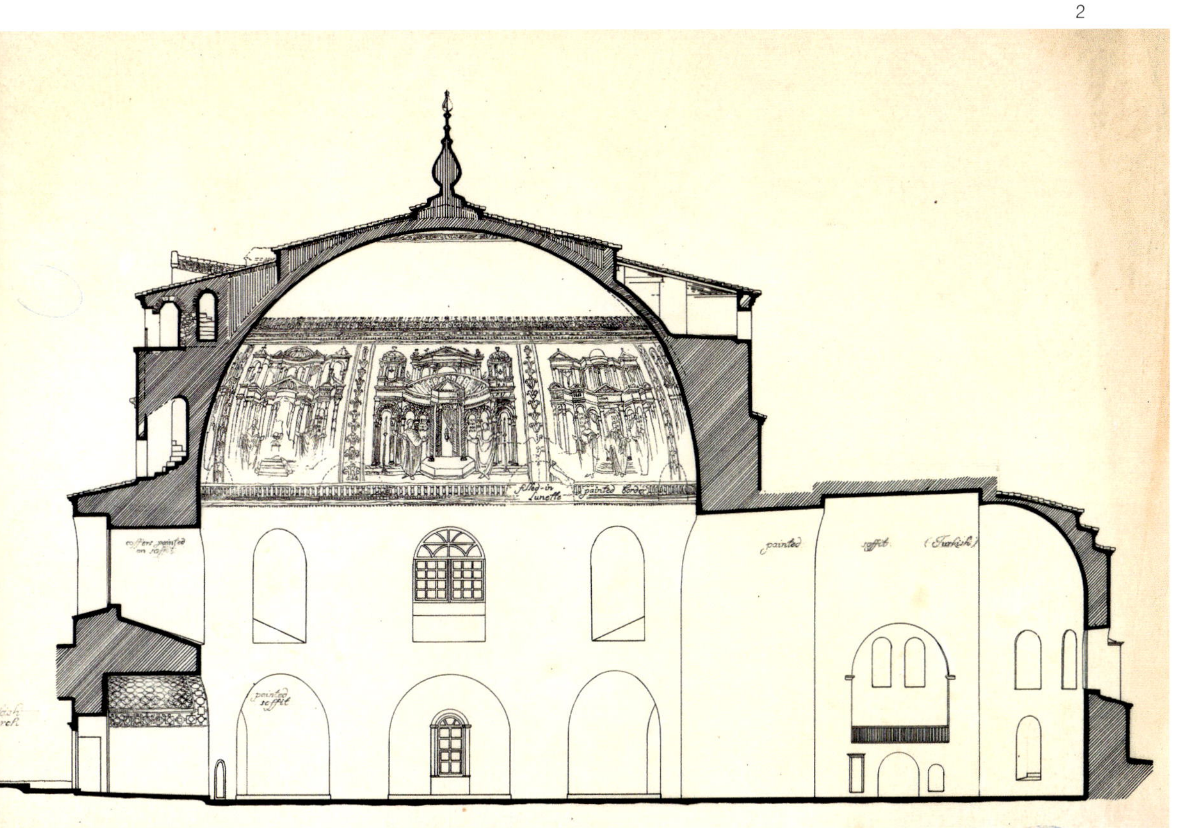

The Roman Rotunda

The Rotunda lies north of the Arch of Galerius, surrounded by tall apartment buildings. As the name implies, it is a circular structure [3]. In fact, with an interior diameter of 24 metres and an exterior diameter of 36.5 metres, the Rotunda is one of the largest centrally-planned buildings remaining from antiquity. It is mainly made of brick reinforced by courses of a local greenstone. At the time of its construction, the 6.3 metre-thick wall, at ground level, was interrupted at regular intervals by eight deep, rectangular barrel-vaulted niches. Of these, the one to the south formed the original entrance. The niches, the large arched windows above them and the smaller openings at the spring of the dome lightened the massive construction.

The Rotunda was enclosed within a walled sacred area, but it formed part of the palace complex that extended from the Rotunda in the north all the way southwards down to the sea. Situated on the main north-south axis of the palatial complex, the Rotunda was connected with the palace by a monumental,

3

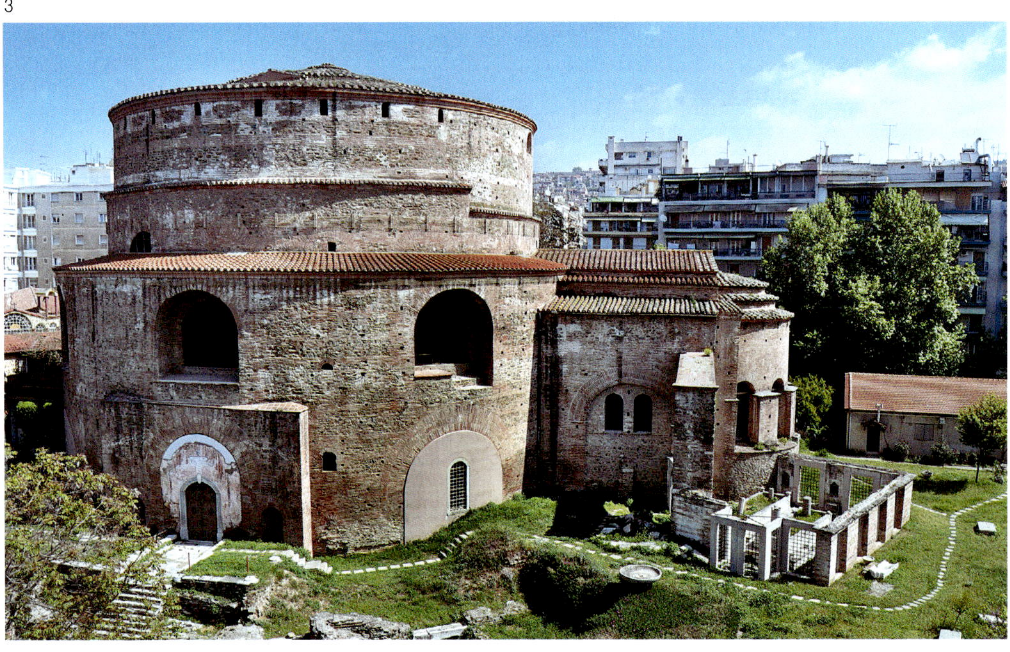

colonnaded processional way and the still-standing triumphal Arch of Galerius (the *Kamara*, of which three of eight piers are preserved) [4]. Just south of the Arch was a great hall (42 × 18m), the so-called *vestibulum* (today covered by the modern Odos Egnatia). From this hall a monumental 18 metre-broad flight of twelve marble steps led down to the palace. The palace area included finely decorated reception halls, such as the still largely preserved Octagon, plus living quarters, courtyards, baths and a large hippodrome.

In the mid-nineteenth century it was believed that the emperor Constantine the Great erected the Rotunda in the 320s (Charles Texier 1849; 1864). A few modern scholars still follow this idea, but the majority of scholars agree that the emperor Galerius (293–311) initiated the construction project. After his victory over the Sasanian Persians led by king Narses in 298 —the victory celebrated by the triumphal arch and its sculpted reliefs— Galerius took up permanent residence in Thessaloniki. The construction of the building may have already started by then, but it is more likely that it began around 305 when Galerius,

3. Exterior view of the Rotunda from the southeast. The door in the south formed the original entrance to the church.

4. Arch of Galerius (Kamara) with Rotunda in the background.

4

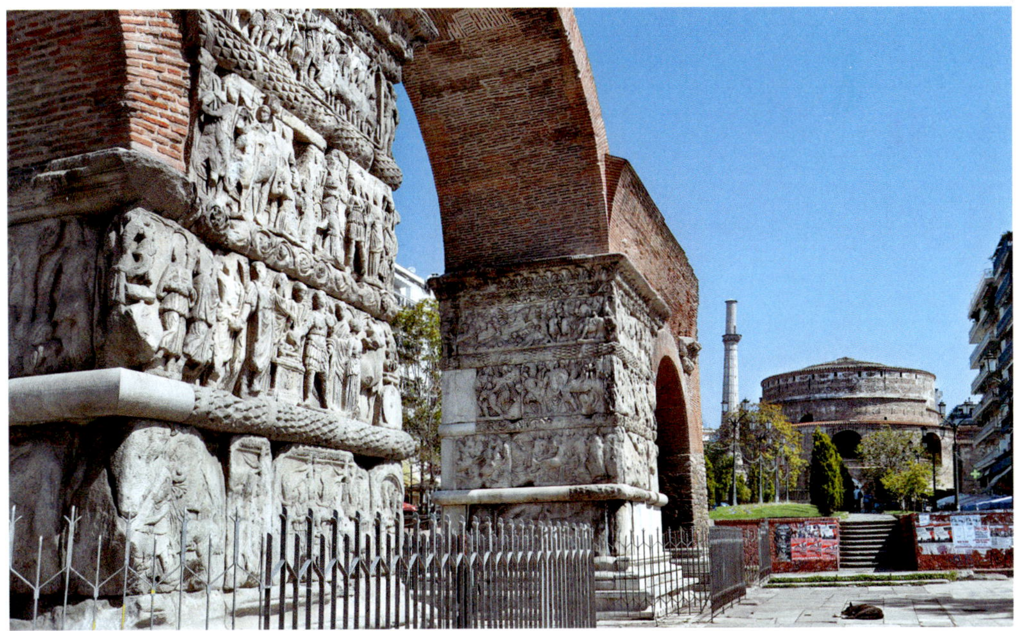

on the death of Diocletian, was raised from *caesar* to the highest imperial rank of *augustus*.

The Roman Rotunda was probably intended to serve as a temple for the imperial cult. It is to some extent comparable in form and function to Hadrian's Pantheon in Rome. When planned, it may also have been intended as Galerius' mausoleum. However, when the emperor died in 311, the Rotunda was still unfinished, and Galerius was buried far from Thessaloniki, in his hometown Romuliana in Illyricum, modern Gamzigrad in Serbia. Coincidentally, Galerius, who had avidly persecuted the Christians, had just signed a decree ordering the toleration of Christianity.

The Conversion into a Church

In a second building phase, the unfinished and probably partly unroofed structure was completed and converted into a centrally-planned, domed church [5]. Today the church is known as the Rotunda of St George, but this name is not attested earlier than the Turkish period. In the Middle Ages it was also called the church of the *Asomatoi* —the Angels— but it was probably originally dedicated to Christ and to the martyrs. At the time of its conversion into a church, the brick dome was finished; the eastern niche was enlarged and extended by the addition of an apsidal choir, while the end walls of the seven other niches were eliminated in order to give access to a wide ambulatory that was added around the building's perimeter. Thus created, the impressive church had a diameter of 54 metres. Following an earthquake in the first half of the sixth century, the church was repaired and an octagonal baptistery was constructed to the west of the entrance (building phase III) [6]. The ambulatory was later destroyed and abandoned, presumably in the vast earthquake that struck the area around 620. This earthquake, which caused serious damage to the building, is described in the *Miracles of St Demetrius*. The niches were subsequently walled-up again — as we see them today.

The date of the building's conversion into a church is highly disputed, with suggestions ranging from the fourth to the sixth

5. Rotunda with processional way, arch and vestibulum (reconstruction Ejnar Dyggve, modified by P. Papagialias).

6. The Rotunda as a church, with octagonal baptistery added in the sixth century (drawing: P. Papagialias).

7. Golden architectural scenery in martyr zone: two-storeyed buildings with arcades and columns. In front of the buildings are saints with their hands raised in prayer.

century (see the section on the date of the mosaics). In our opinion, the conversion was instigated by Theodosius I (379–395), who wanted the building to serve as his palace church. To use an existing, partly finished monument was obviously time-saving, but the plausible main reason for choosing this particular building was its topographical situation: it was the only available centralized structure in the palace area that offered sufficient space for erecting a church of such exceptional dimensions; the site allowed the original circular structure to be augmented with a large choir and a wide ambulatory.

In connection with the conversion, the interior surfaces of the walls and floors were clad in white and coloured marble slabs. These marble revetments are unfortunately no longer preserved; all we have are minuscule fragments (attested in photos, but the present whereabouts are uncertain). Nevertheless, with an inner diameter of more than 24 metres and a height of about 29 metres to the zenith of the cupola, the Rotunda is a truly magnificent space. The original floor lay about 1 metre below the modern floor, so the interior volume was even more impressive in antiquity. It must have been a wondrous sight when the walls and floors clad in shining marble revetments and with the usual church furnishings such as chandeliers, lamps and incense burners were viewed together with the glittering golden and silver mosaics [7].

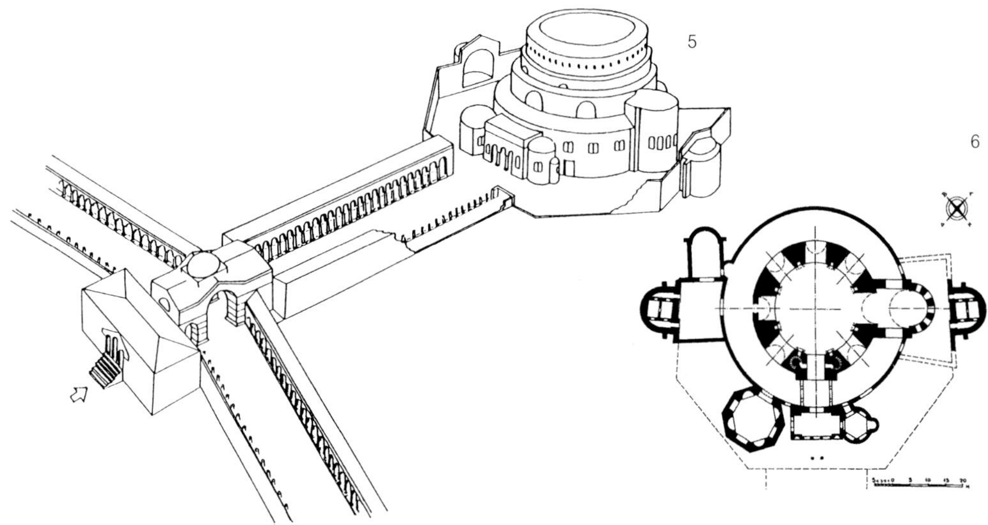

7

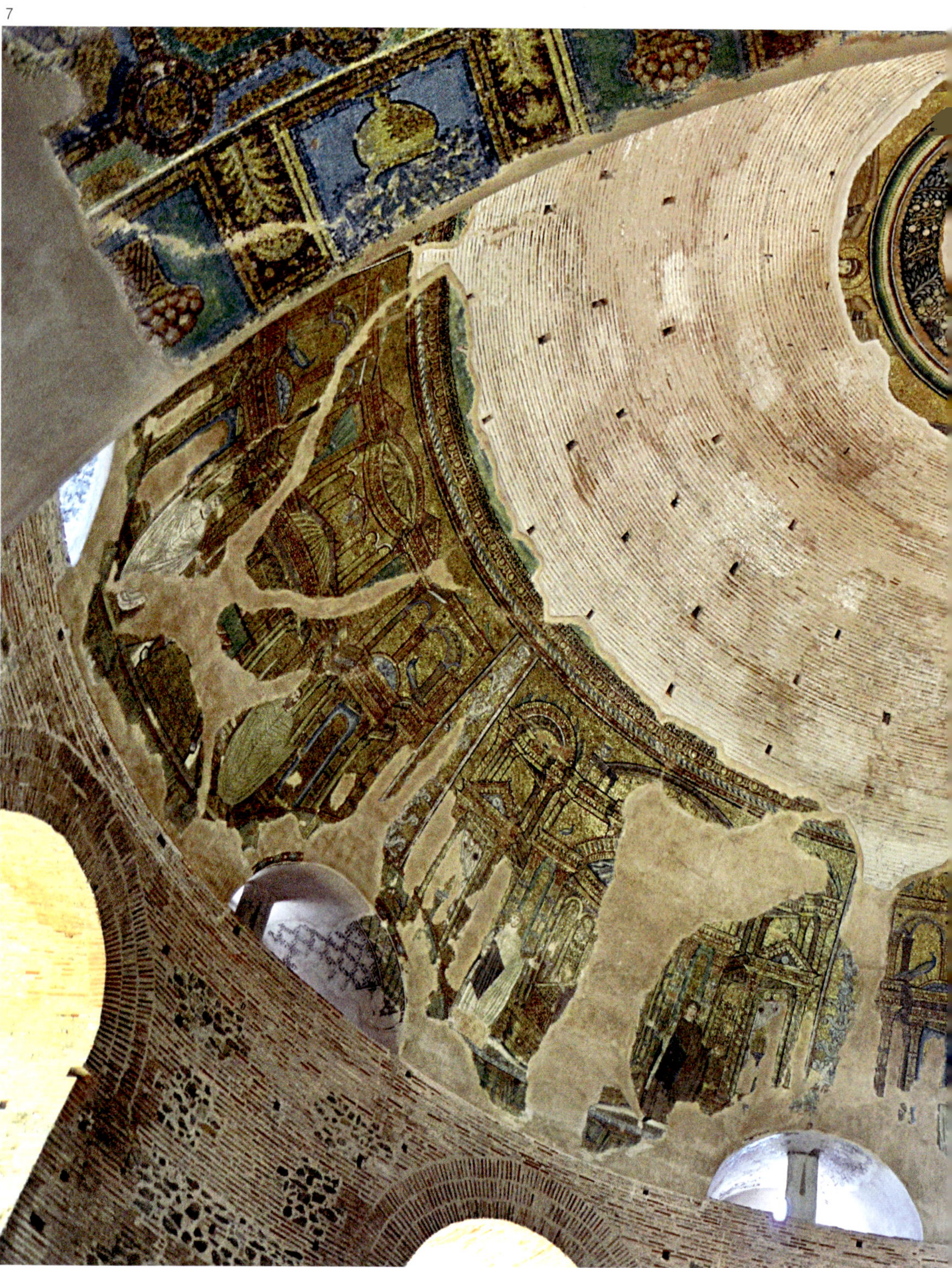

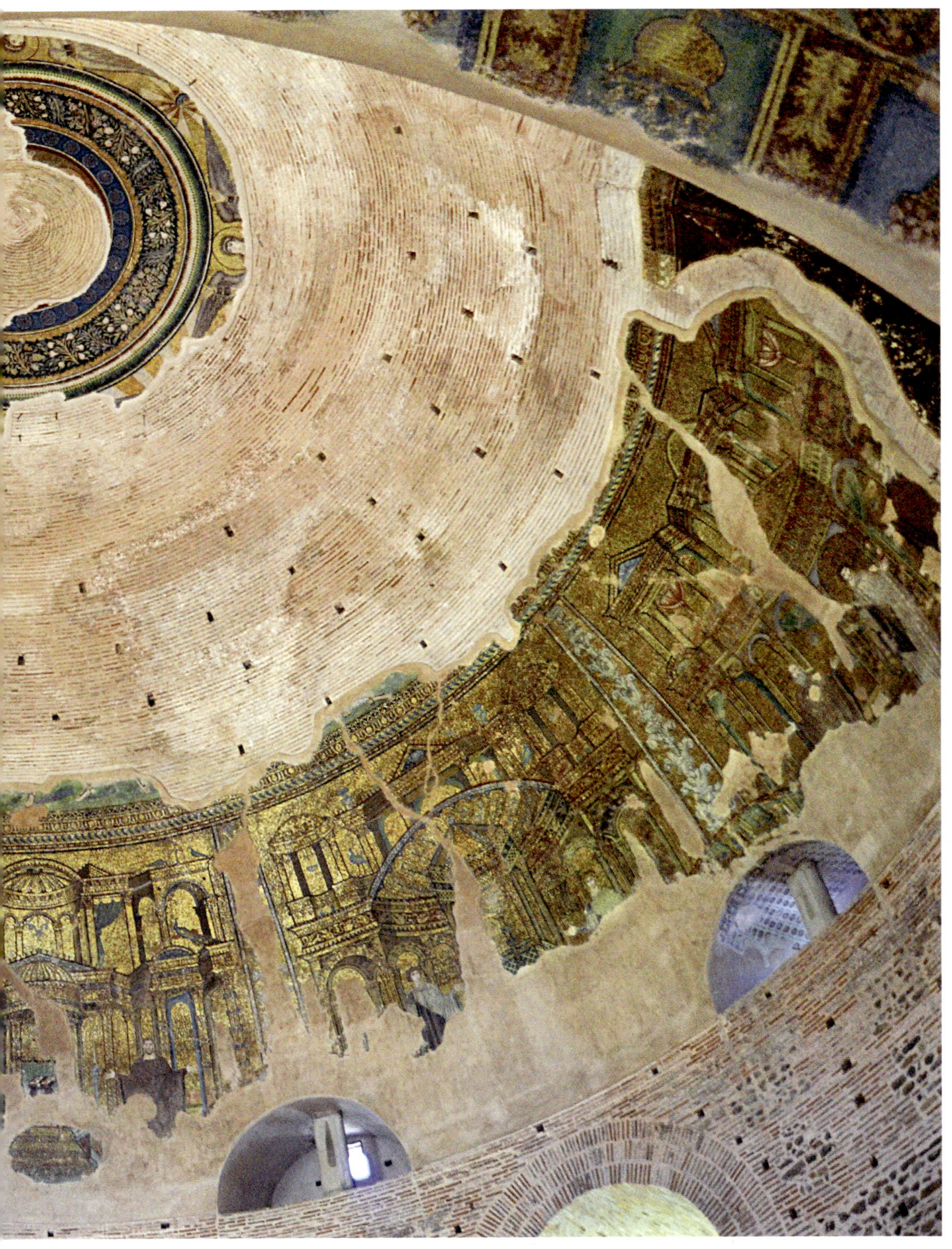

Overview of the Mosaic Decorations

Before discussing the iconographic and aesthetic characteristics of the Rotunda mosaics, a short overview of the decorations will give an idea of the general layout. Mosaics originally covered the entire cupola and the barrel vaults of passages and windows. Fortunately, important parts of these mosaic decorations have withstood the calamities of time, of which earthquakes have taken the greatest toll.

The mosaics in the cupola are arranged in three superimposed zones forming a unified pictorial programme. At the summit, the central medallion contained an image of Christ. The extant try-out or preparatory sketch reveals that he appeared in a long flowing robe. Fragments of mosaic show that Christ stood out against the shimmering light reflecting from large silver tesserae. The divine image is framed by three concentric bands: a circle of silver stars on a blue ground, a garland of fruit, flowers and evergreen plants, and, surrounding this again, the band of a colourful rainbow [38]. The head of Phoenix can be seen under the rainbow, while, to the north, rays emanate from a now lost cross. The medallion with Christ is supported by four large hovering angels dressed in white flowing robes (see pp. 46–52).

Below the medallion, the middle zone of the cupola is now a vast area of brickwork almost devoid of mosaic. The bare areas and the cracks in the masonry give evidence of the many earthquakes that over the centuries have damaged the building. Mosaic fragments (to the south and north-west) of sandal-clad feet on a green field indicate that this zone was inhabited by a large number of more than 3 metre-tall figures, perhaps around thirty or even more [9]. Dressed in white like the hovering angels above, it is reasonable to assume that these figures were also angels. This interpretation is strengthened by the fact that from the early Middle Ages, the church was known as the sanctuary of the *Asomatoi* (*naos ton Asomaton*) the incorporeal beings, the angels. Judging from the

8. The martyr Therinos.

8

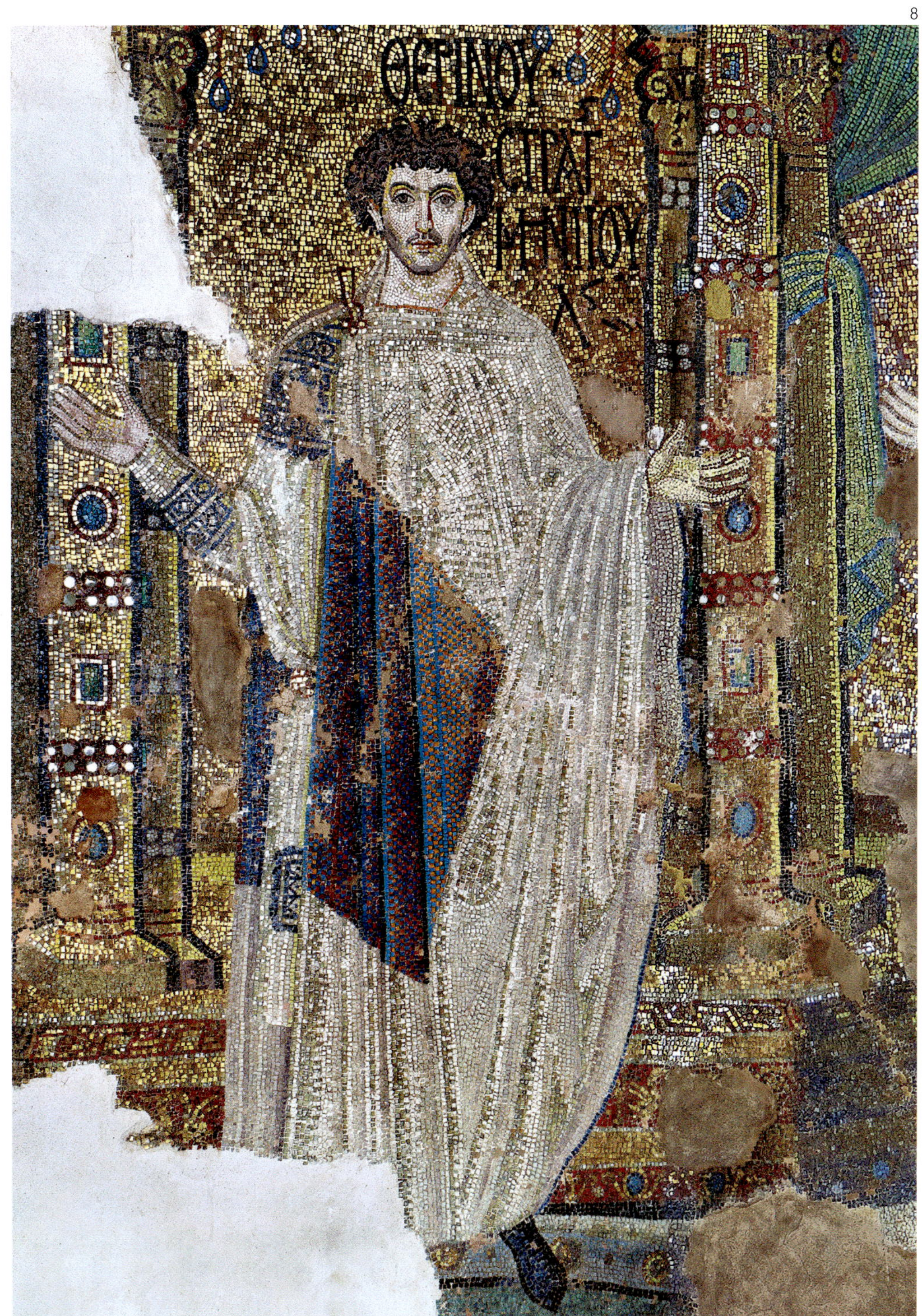

9

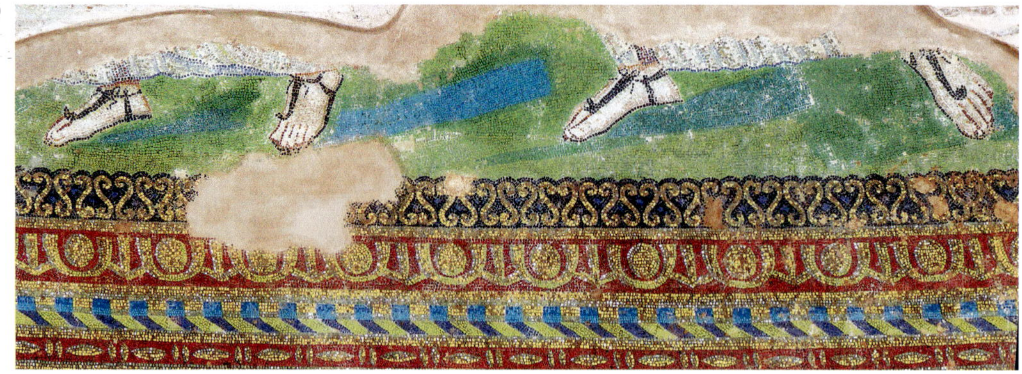

9. Sandal-clad feet remaining of angels in the lost middle zone of the cupola. About twenty-eight to thirty more than 3-metre tall figures in motion were originally presented here.

10. Vegetal mosaics in the eastern light opening showing lilies and fruit.

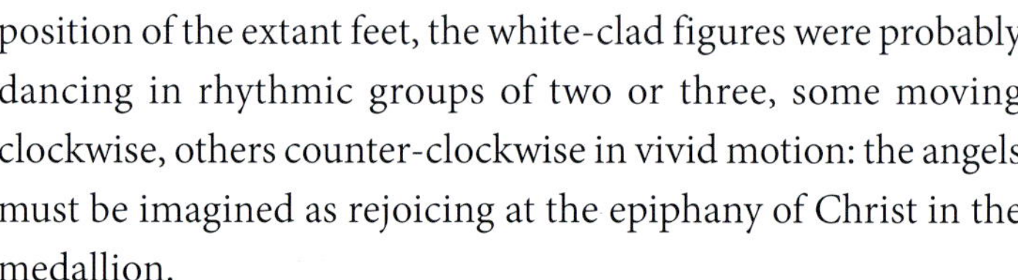

position of the extant feet, the white-clad figures were probably dancing in rhythmic groups of two or three, some moving clockwise, others counter-clockwise in vivid motion: the angels must be imagined as rejoicing at the epiphany of Christ in the medallion.

The lowest zone of the cupola (*ca* 8 m high, mosaic frames included) is preserved in most of its splendour with gold-glittering architectural scenery set against a golden ground. The zone is divided into eight panels. The one to the east, above the choir, is lost; it was possibly destroyed in the vast earthquake around 620. The mosaic panel is replaced by a now darkened painted imitation. Each of the eight panels depicts golden two-storeyed buildings with *ciboria* (canopies), arcades, pediments and columns. In front of the buildings are two or three saints with their hands lifted in the gesture of prayer [7] (see pp. 30–42).

10

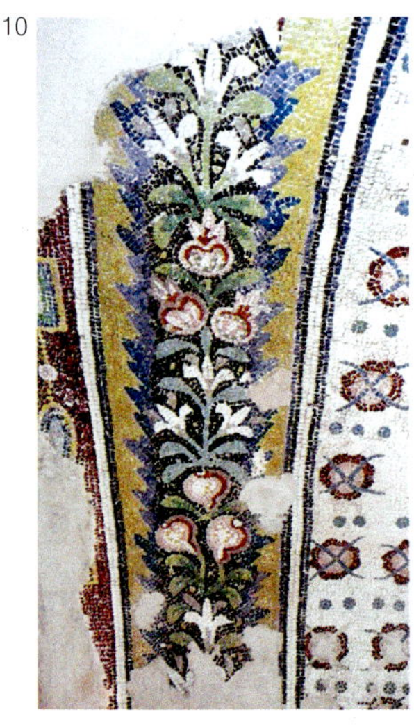

Vaulted light openings at the base of the cupola lighten the heavy architecture. Six of these openings still contain mosaics displaying variations on floral, vegetal and geometrical designs [10]. The technique used here is related to that of Hellenistic and Roman floor mosaics. Gold and silver tesserae have not been used, as the mosaics were not meant to reflect but to transmit the incoming daylight. While one could see such non-figural mosaics simply as ornamental, it can be assumed that these very fine, mosaic-laid areas represent the beauty and abundance of nature, a theme stressed in the larger barrel vaults.

11

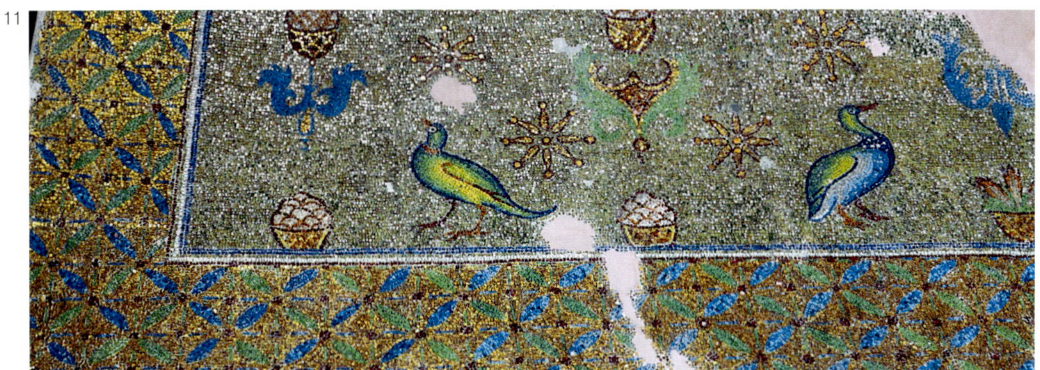

Mosaics are preserved in three of the seven barrel vaults. The vault to the south, which was the original entranceway through which the emperor entered his palace church, is particularly splendid [11, 14–15]. A large golden cross is set in the centre of a shimmering silver field gleaming with stars, birds, baskets, stylized flowers and acanthus leaves. The particular importance of this vault is emphasized by the fact that besides the medallion at the zenith of the cupola, it is the only one with a silver ground. Like the medallion with the figure of Christ, the mosaic depicts an epiphany — here, however, in the form of the cross (see pp. 20–21).

12

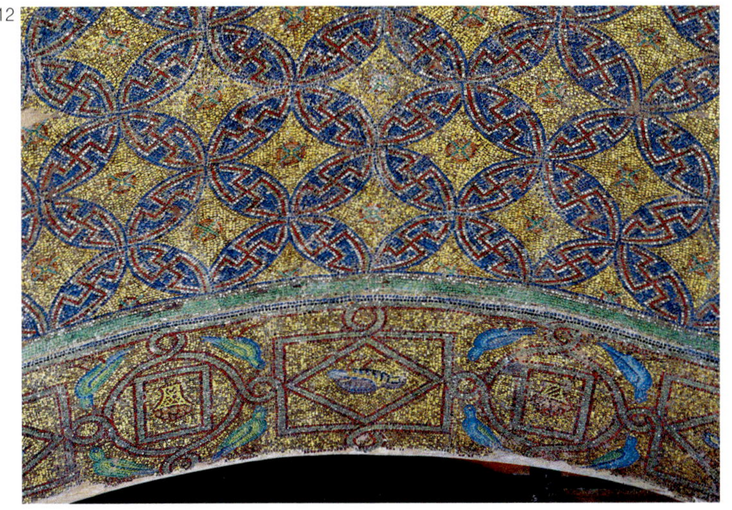

11. Silver mosaic with birds and baskets, entrance vault, south. It gives an impression of a silk textile.

12. Detail of mosaics in blue, red and silver interlace on a gold ground designed to look like a carpet with "fringe" in the western vault (current entrance to the Rotunda).

13. Golden compartments with birds and fruit in the southeast vault. The design reproduces a coffered ceiling.

The western vault —under which the visitor today enters the building— is laid out like a silk carpet with a uniform design of intersecting circles in blue, red and silver set against a golden background. The textile quality of this mosaic is strengthened by a border designed to imitate a row of fringe. A golden frieze of birds alternating with baskets frames the mosaic running below the fringe and along the arch openings [12].

The southeast vault is divided into golden octagonal compartments each decorated with either a bird or a fruit, beautifully designed in strong colours of blue, turquoise, green, red and yellow. The square sunken panels of the border contain images of vases and baskets filled with flowers. While the extant mosaics in the two other vaults give an impression of silk textiles, the mosaic imagery in this vault clearly reproduces a coffered ceiling [13].

13

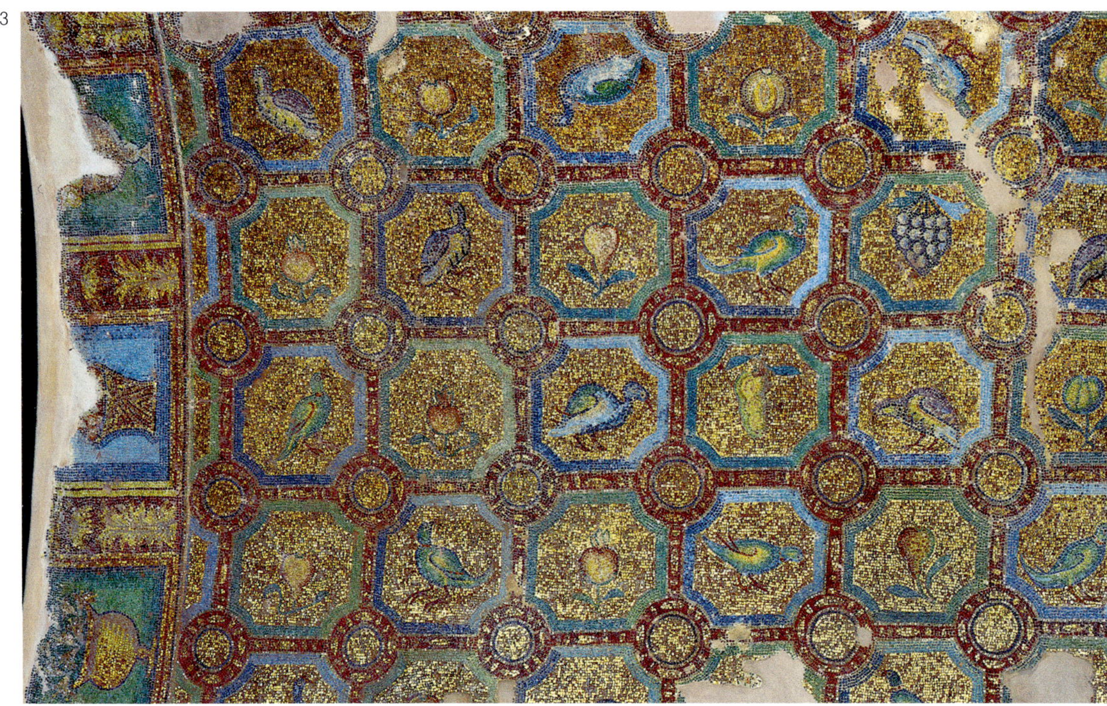

The Date of the Mosaics

No ancient documents mention the erection of the Rotunda, its conversion into a church or its decoration with mosaics. The date of the mosaics is therefore unknown and highly disputed. In current scholarship, suggested dates range from the early fourth to the early sixth century. Since there are no stylistic or iconographic parallels to these extraordinary mosaics, the controversy over their chronology is unsurprising.

The Rotunda is situated on the grounds of the Roman and early Christian palace, and it is logical to assume that an emperor was the principal force behind the project of converting and decorating the building. This emperor has been variously identified as Constantine the Great (307–337), Theodosius the Great (379–395), or Theodosius' daughter Galla Placidia, who spent the winter of 424–425 in Thessaloniki. The scholars who argue that the mosaics date from the mid-fifth to the early sixth century have failed to come up with the name of a potential commissioner. The conversion of the building into a church of exceptional dimensions, the furnishing and especially the laying of the mosaics required vast economic resources. Since the empress Galla Placidia, who was in exile from the Western Roman Empire when she was in Thessaloniki, had neither legal nor financial power in the Eastern Empire, she would not have been in a position to organize and finance this ambitious project.

Theodosius the Great was the last late antique emperor to stay in Thessaloniki for longer periods of time. He resided there first from January 379 to November 380, then again in 387–388 and subsequently for various shorter or longer stays. In January 388 he celebrated his *decennalia*, ten year anniversary as emperor, and married the princess Galla (Galla Placidia's mother) in Thessaloniki. Theodosius visited Thessaloniki again in 391 and 394. A true believer who in 391 made Christianity the sole legal religion of the Roman Empire, Theodosius could hardly have done without a palace church. His faith must have been further strengthened when, in his first year in Thessaloniki, he fell seriously ill but then, after being baptized, miraculously recovered. Theodosius therefore had good reasons for executing this mega-project, and from a historical, juridical and economic point of view, he is the most likely candidate. As will be discussed (in the section on dogmatic themes), some of the iconographic motifs may actually refer to Theodosius' religious policy.

The Silver Vault

Imagine the imperial entourage as it leaves from the palace to the south, passes through the triumphal arch and along the processional way and finally arrives at the Rotunda. Entering the Rotunda, the first mosaics the emperor encounters are those in the barrel vault over the southern monumental entranceway. As noted, this decoration stands out for being set on a silver ground: except for the medallion of Christ at the top of the cupola, all the remaining mosaics are set against a golden ground. The emperor thus finds this glimmering silver *baldacchino* (canopy) spread above his head [15]. A large golden cross glitters in its centre. The emperor —like the modern visitor— sees a vision of the cross, a gleaming *staurophania*.

14 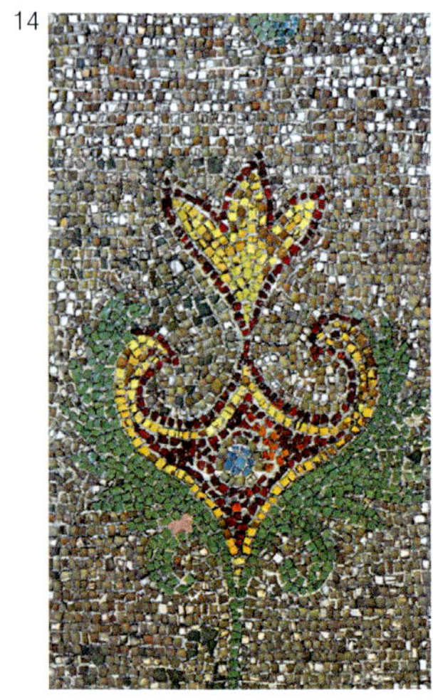

14. Silver vault, detail of pelta-shield with acanthus leaves.

15. Silver vault, south, showing large gold cross against a shimmering silken ground with birds, gold baskets, leaves and gold stars.

The cross is surrounded by pheasants, ducks, stars, flowers and baskets, all laid out in a regular repeat pattern. The mosaic looks like a rich silk textile, and the first impression is of Sasanian silk [14]. Multi-coloured silks imported from the East were in fashion at the court. Several pictorial motifs in the mosaic bring to mind Sasanian art, especially the wing-shaped blue and green acanthus leaves. But most of the imagery is also found in Roman imperial sculpture and painting. For instance, the eagle-headed pelta-shield is a typical Roman motif. Birds and stars are also common in both the Western and Eastern empires. The mosaics are therefore open to several interpretations. There seems to be a mixture of western and eastern elements, including a subtle allusion to the Persians, the traditional enemies of the Roman State.

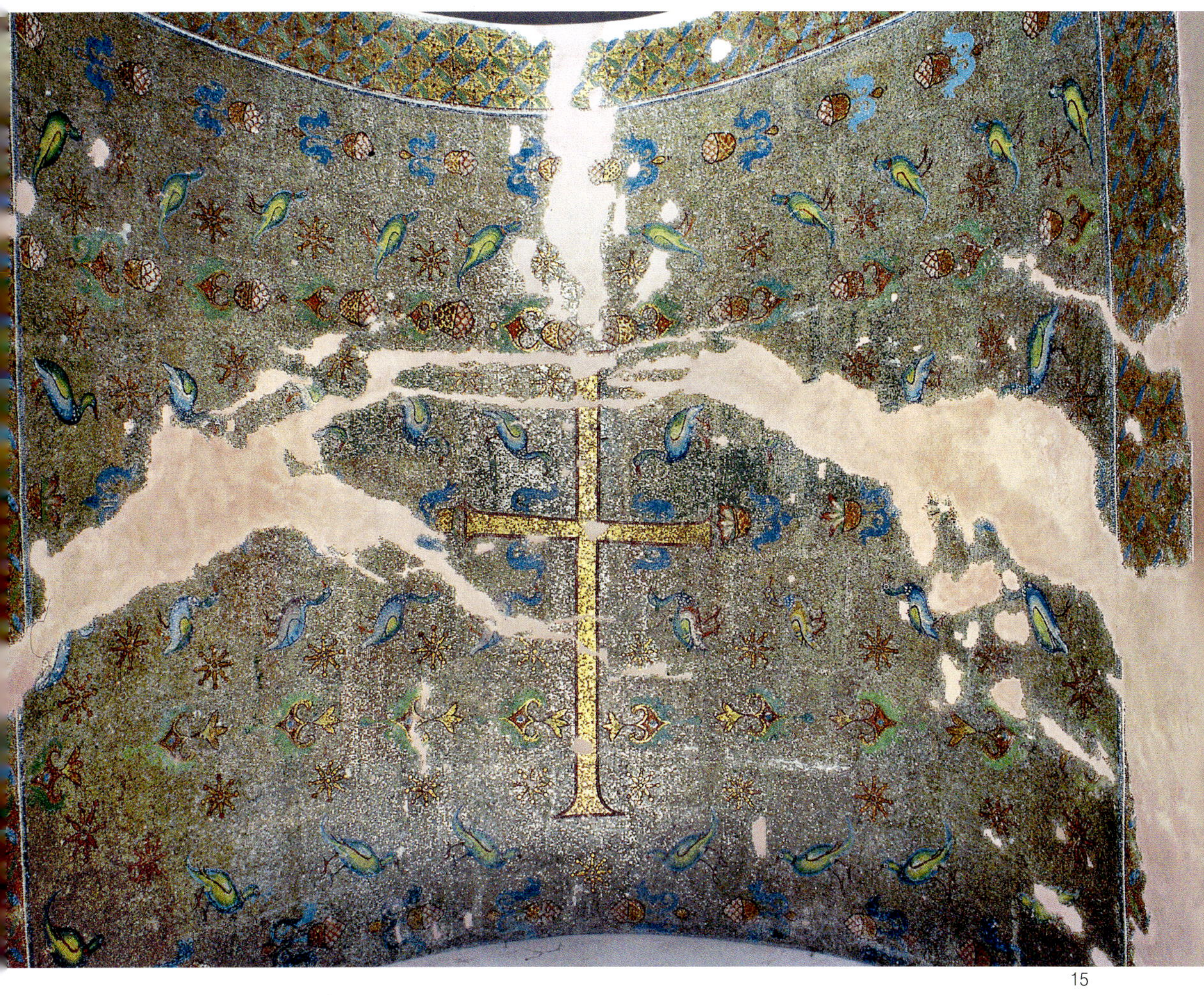

15

We can link the decoration of the entranceway vault to the triumphal arch of Galerius, 130 metres south of the Rotunda. On the lower part of the arch, Sasanian Persians bring the emperor gifts in the form of silk textiles and golden cups [16]. The reliefs were undoubtedly painted, following common practice in antiquity, so their motifs would have been further highlighted in colour. The cross and the other motifs in the entrance-vault mosaic may therefore contain a message not only of religious but also of political significance.

16. Sasanians bringing the emperor gifts in the form of silk textiles and golden cups. Relief, Arch of Galerius.

17. Vertical frame of architectural zone; acanthus lesene. Eight lesenes decorated with white acanthus divide the architectural zone into eight panels.

18. Architectural zone with martyrs: the soldier Onesiphoros and his companion Porphyrios.

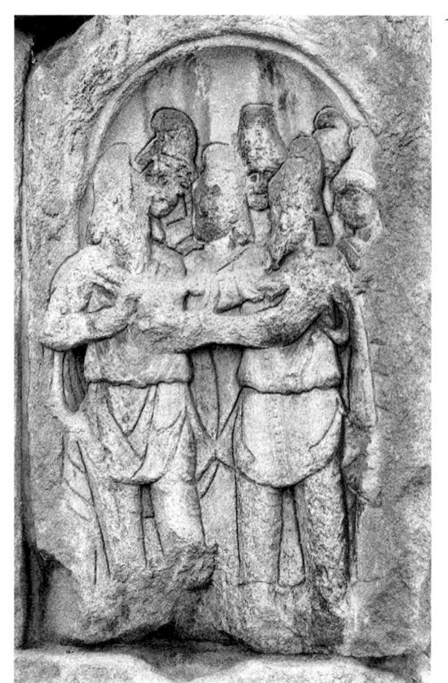
16

The Martyr Zone

THE GOLDEN ARCHITECTURE

Having entered the church from the south, the emperor would have caught sight of the splendid mosaics in the cupola. The architectural zone encircling the cupola is laid out as a vast panorama framed by elaborate borders [18]. The frame below marks the transition from the mosaics in the cupola to the no-longer-extant marble revetments on the cylindrical wall. It is particularly elaborately designed, like a modillion cornice with console-supports and arches [17]. Along its lowest border is a gemmed band. This composite frame runs the entire length along the panels and around the edges of the vaulted light openings. The border above the architectural zone is laid out as a cornice consisting of a double-S frieze, an Ionic cymatium and a three-dimensional dentil frieze. Both the upper and the lower borders are designed to give the illusion of sculpted architecture.

Eight lesenes (pilasters without capitals and bases) divide the architectural zone into eight large panels. Each lesene is decorated with a large white acanthus outlined in blue and originally interspersed with silver [17]. Since the acanthuses are designed to look like marble reliefs, the lesenes may be a continuation of pilaster motifs from the marble revetment on the lower part of the walls. But the precise layout of the revetment is uncertain, as all that remain *in situ* are holes for fastening the marble slabs.

The architecture depicted in the mosaics is truly impressive. Some of the elements reflect real buildings, but they are transformed into heavenly structures of gold with silver highlights set off against the golden background by black, red or ultramarine contours [19]. The projecting and receding elements vary in design, but all panels are two-storeyed and centralized with a circular *tholos* or an octagonal ciborium as the focal point. Some columns are spirally fluted; others are inlaid with pearls and gems. The pictured entablatures and pediments are richly ornamented. Friezes and bands show about thirty different designs: bands of gems and precious stones, friezes with silver *peltae* (ornamental Amazon shields) and simpler ornaments deriving from classical architecture. One particularly fine frieze in red and gold depicts symmetrically arranged swans with bent necks [21]. A few peacocks —like the Phoenix symbols of rebirth and eternity— and other birds perch on pediments [20]. Vases and *thymiateria* (incense burners) are other visual accents that define the space as holy. All in all, the architectural zone presents a vision of light and splendour.

The golden structures pictured in the Rotunda mosaics have no equivalent in Christian art. In the cupola of the Orthodox baptistery at Ravenna, dating from the 450s, a rudimentary architecture is represented by garden-like pavilions, but it is not comparable to the monumentality and splendour of the Rotunda's architectural imagery. In the Rotunda mosaics, the design of the two-storeyed buildings with ciboria, pearl-and-gem studded columns and birds is comparable to Roman painting of the second and fourth Pompeian styles. Just as in these wall paintings, the mosaics' differing perspectives result in multiple viewpoints: some parts of the design are seen from below, others at eye level. These various perspectives render the mosaic scenery particularly

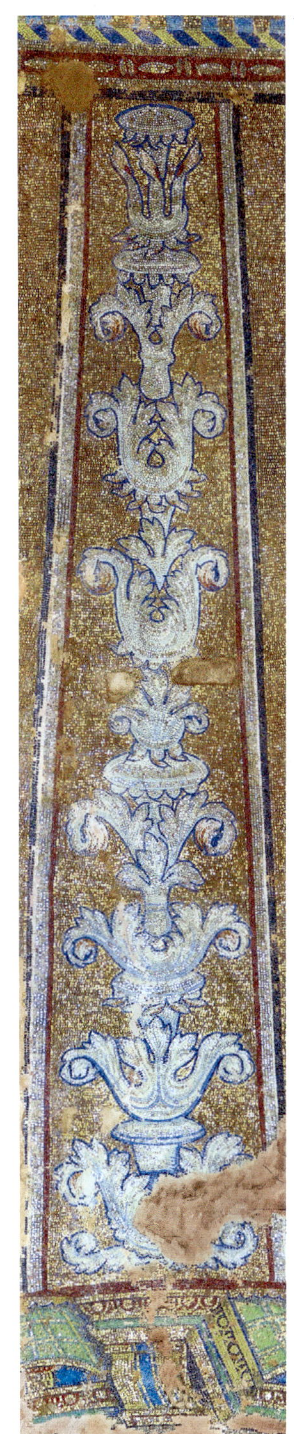
17

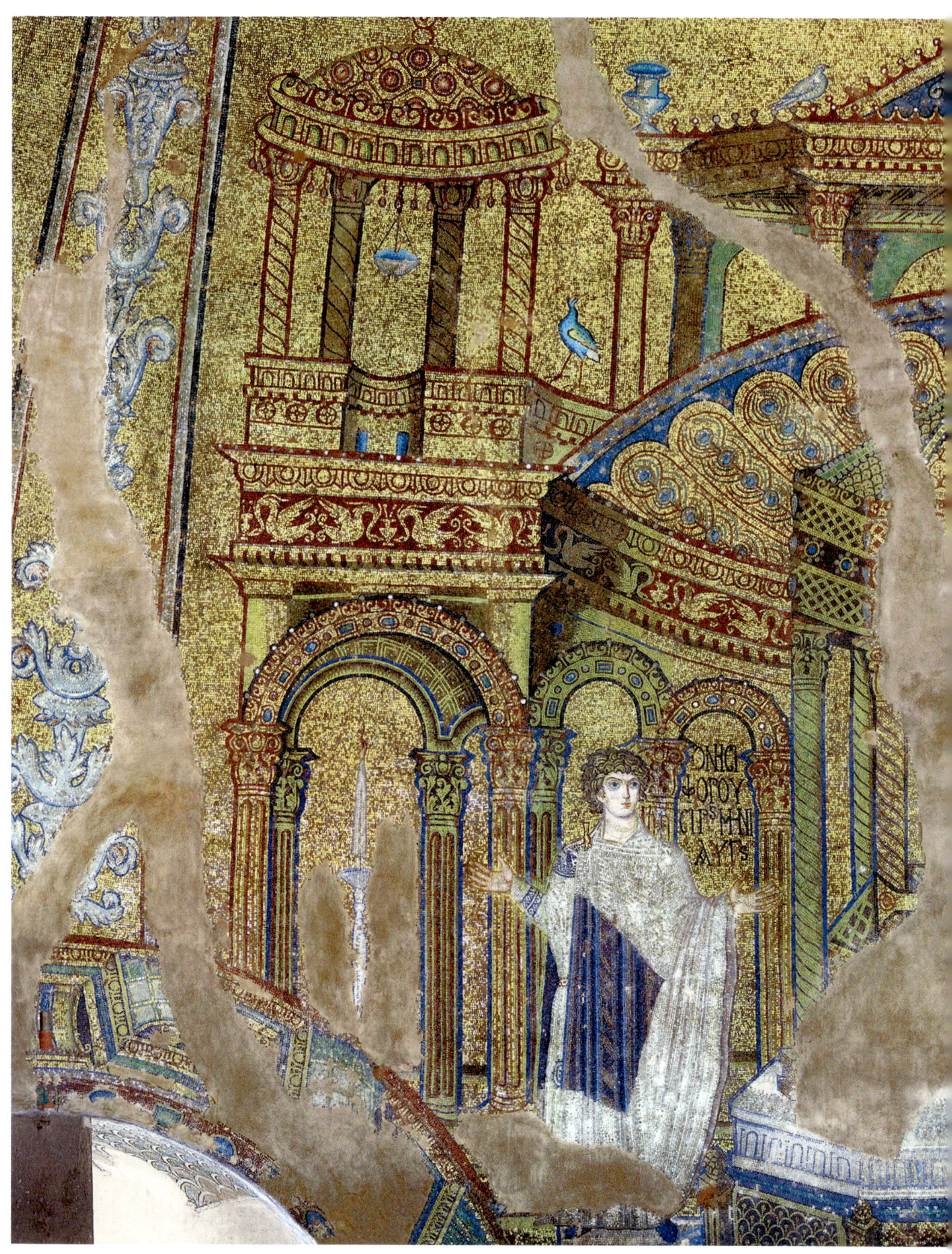
ΟΝΗϹΙ
ΦΟΡΟΥ

18

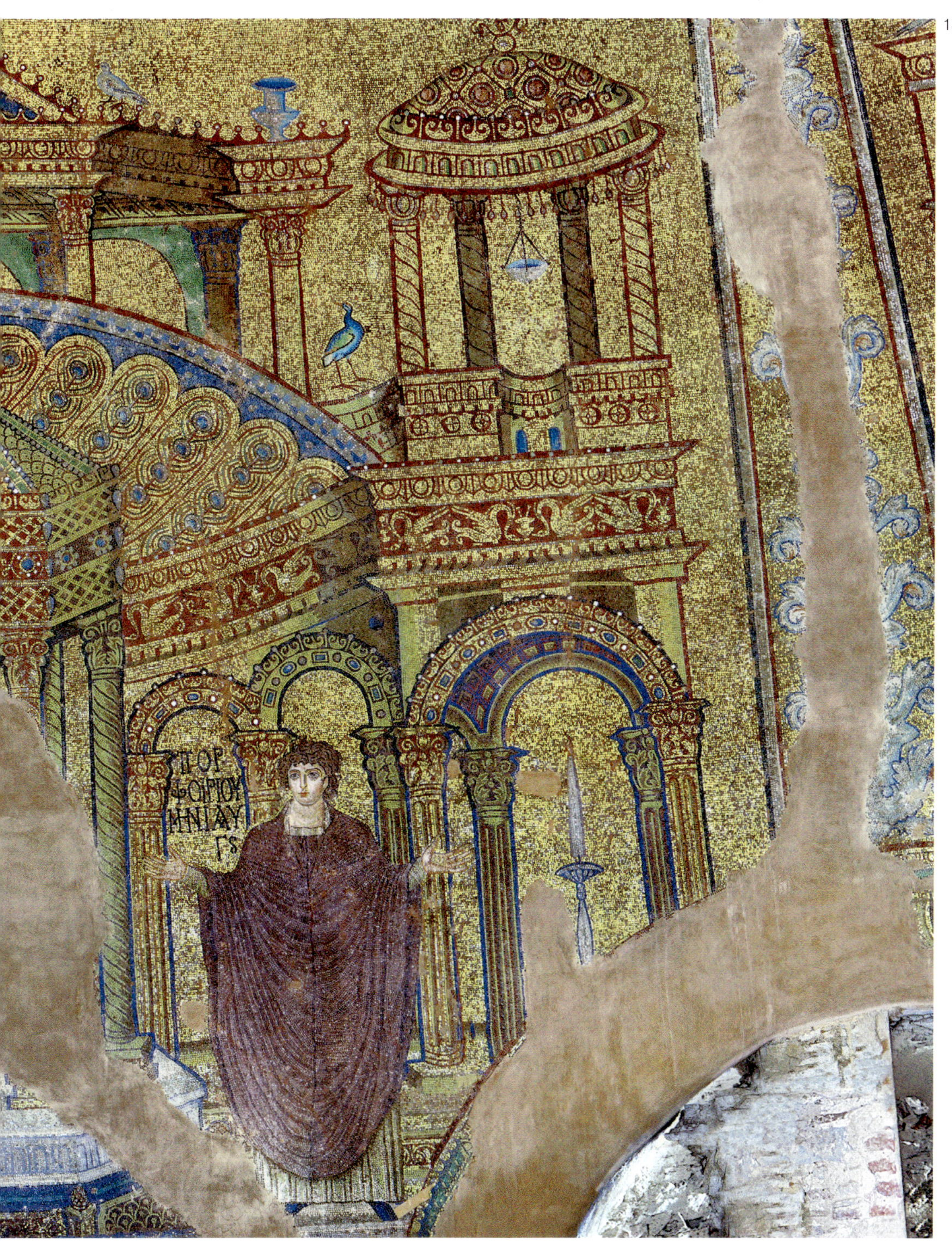

19

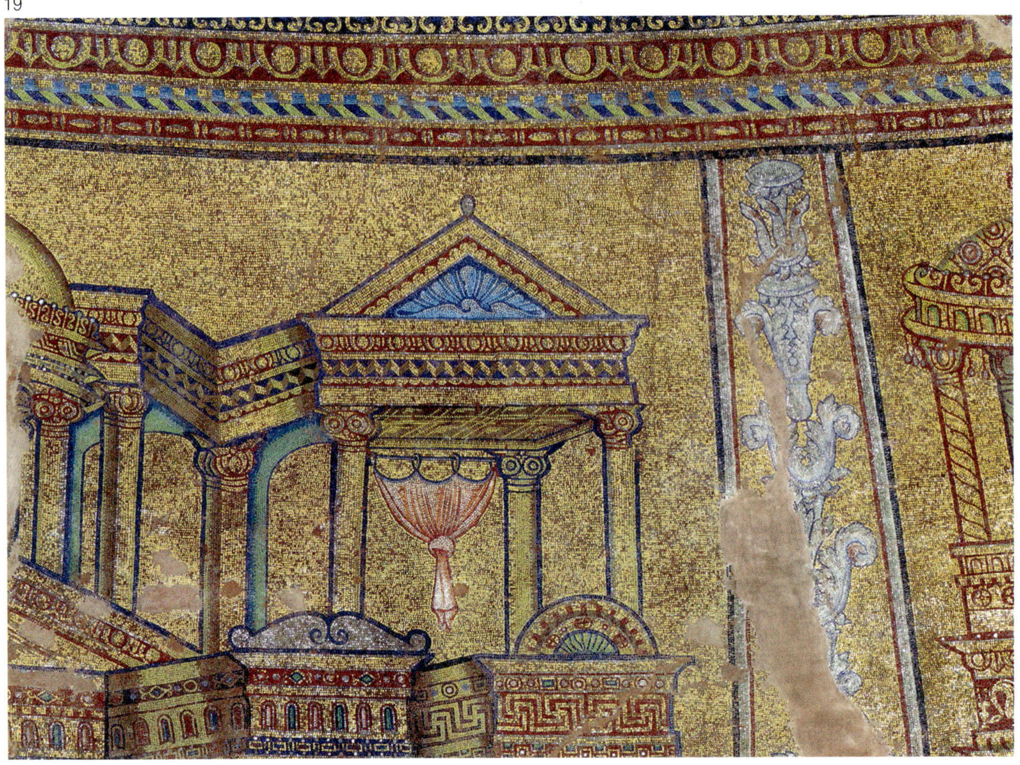

20

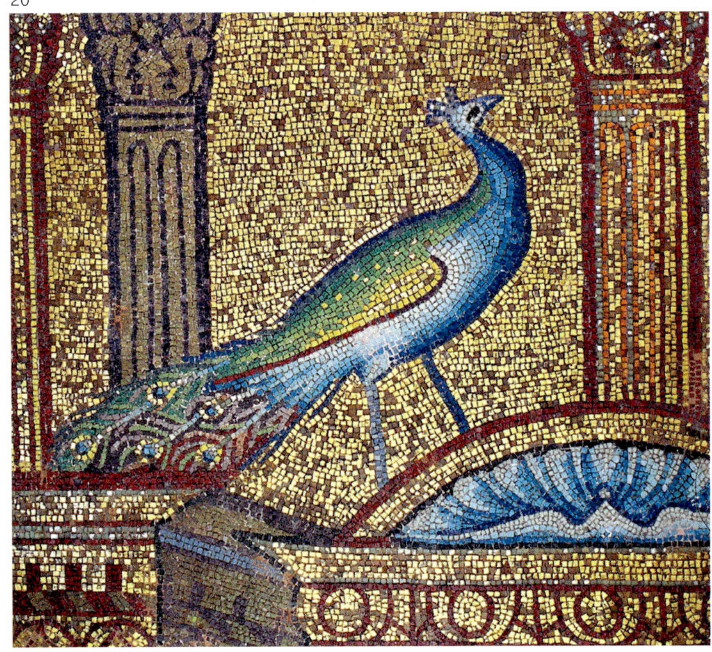

21

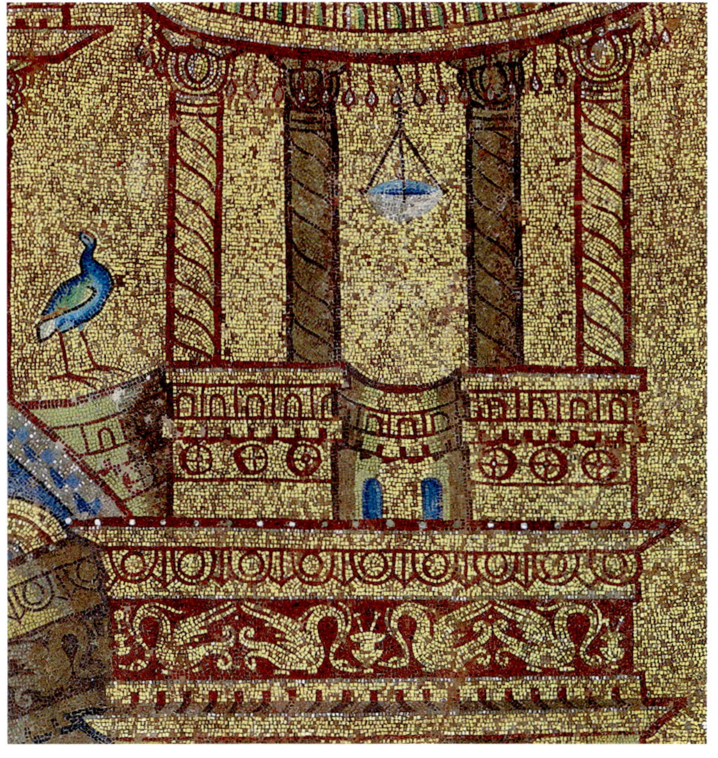

19. Detail of golden structures in the martyr zone depicting golden buildings set against a golden ground.

20. Detail of architecture with peacock, a symbol of rebirth and eternity.

21. Detail of architecture with swan frieze in red and gold.

22. The physician martyrs Kosmas and Damian stand in front of the golden architecture. They flank a codex displayed on a finely adorned chair placed on top of a stepped podium.

intriguing. The structures in the Rotunda also display features shared by the monumental rock-cut façades at Petra in Jordan: the central *tholos* and the split pediment indicate that the rock-cut façades and the mosaic images stem from a common Hellenistic tradition, reflecting a palatial setting.

The architecture depicted in the Rotunda surely has specific significance. Derived from the stage-set (*scaenae frons*) architecture, it is a scenography that can take on different meanings depending on the figures that inhabit it. In Hellenistic wall decorations, the presence of rulers signifies that the depicted architecture is a palace. When Jupiter, Apollo and other gods inhabit it, as in Roman wall paintings, the signified location is Olympus, the home of the gods. Inhabited by saints, as in the Rotunda, it is the abode of the just, the heavenly Jerusalem. In the Rotunda mosaics, the presence of the saints determines the celestial meaning of the architectural setting.

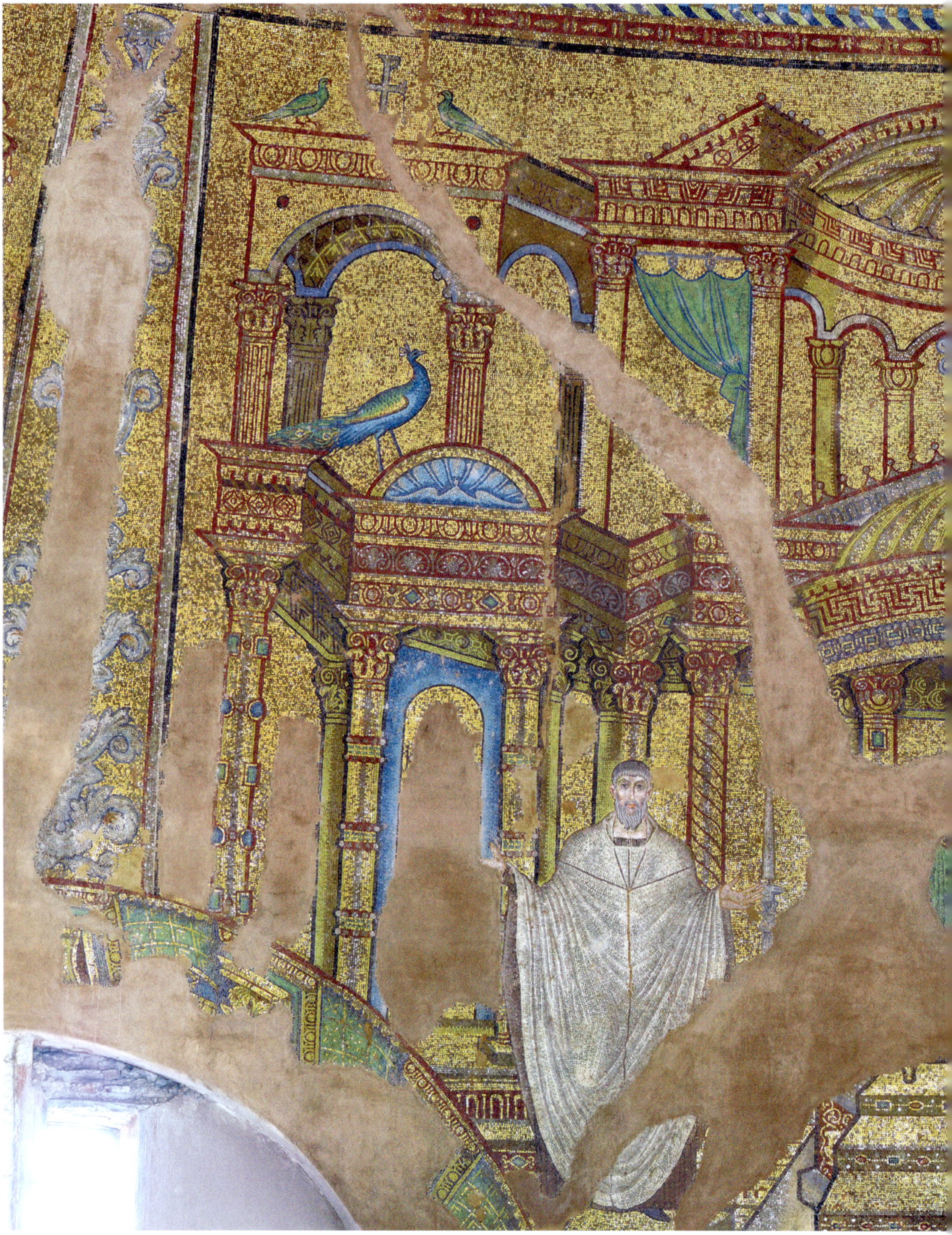

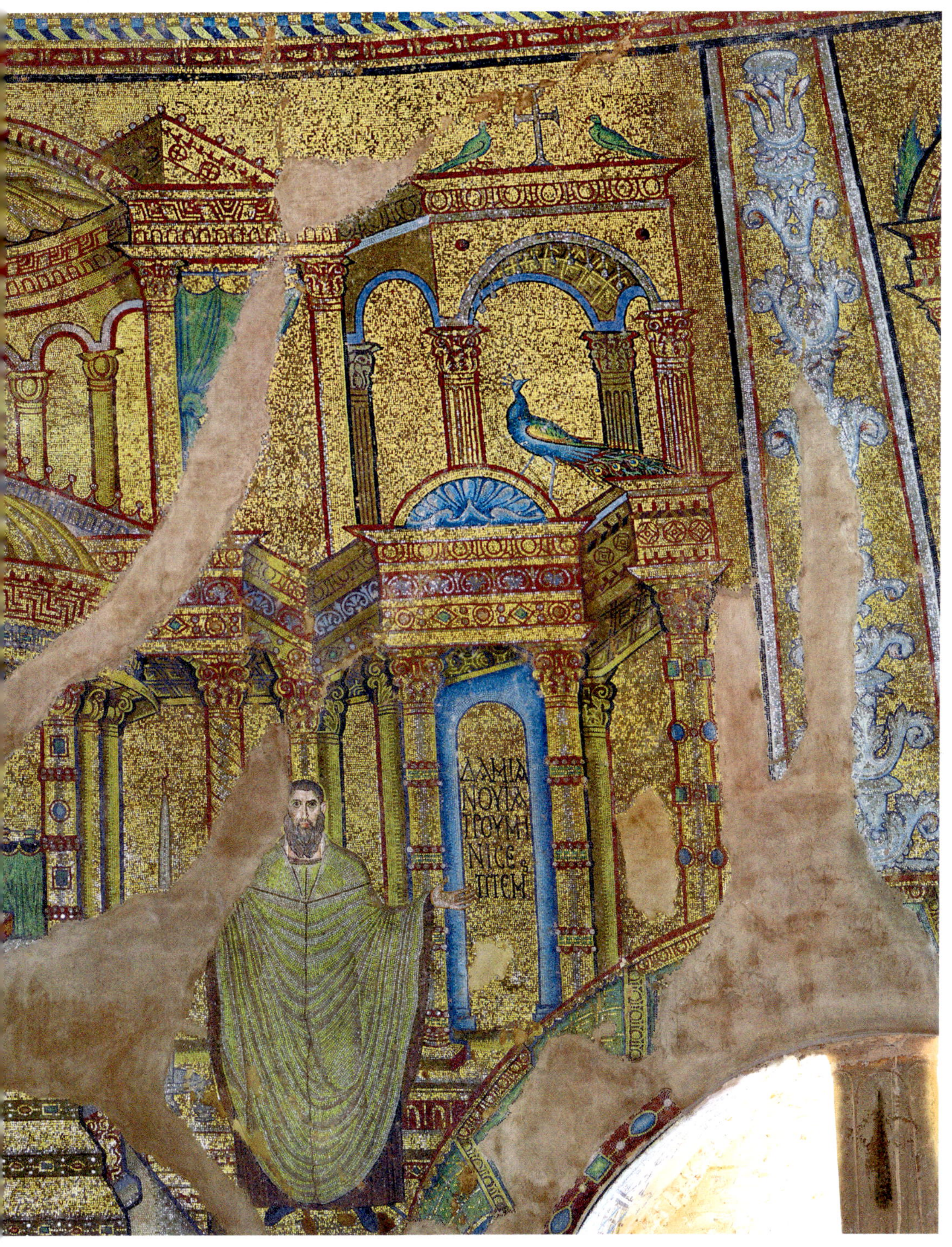
ΔΑΜΙΑ

THE MARTYRS

In front of each golden architectural panel, either two or three martyrs stand with their hands raised in prayer [22]. Twenty saints were originally present in the mosaics. Fifteen of these are more or less well preserved. Of the fully preserved saints, their height varies from 2.28 to 2.40 metres, measured from the tip of the shoes to the top of the head, hair included. It is thus worth noting that in the period when the mosaics of the saints were made, the artists had not yet developed canonical proportional norms.

Each saint is accompanied by an inscription written in black capital letters, stating his name (in the genitive case), profession (also in the genitive case) and festal month (in the dative case). It goes forth from the inscriptions that the martyrs include ecclesiastics, soldiers and laymen. From east (E) to west (W), moving clockwise from the choir, they are:

ΛΕΟΝΤΟς ΣΤΡΑΤ ΜΗΝΙ ΙΟΥΝ, "of Leon, soldier, month of June" [cf. 31]; ΦΙΛΗΜΟΝΟς ΧΟΡΑΥΛΟΥ ΜΗΝΙ ΜΑΡΤ, "of Philemon, flute-player, month of March" (SE).

ΟΝΗΣΙΦΟΡΟΥ ΣΤΡ ΜΗΝΙ ΑΥΓ, "of Onesiphoros, soldier, month of August"; ΠΟΡΦΟΙΡΙΟΥ ΜΗΝΙ ΑΥΓ, "of Porphyrios, month of August" (S).

ΔΑΜΙΑΝΟΥ ΙΑΤΡΟΥ ΜΗΝΙ ΣΕΠΤΕΜ, "of Damian, physician, month of September". Since Damian is normally presented along with his brother Kosmas, it can be deduced that the only remaining letter 'K' of his companion's name should be read as Kosmas (SW).

The inscription relating to the young blond soldier is lost; in the case of Romanos, only the inscription ΡΩΜΑΝΟΥ ΠΡΕΣΒ, "of Romanos presbyter" is preserved, while the figure of Romanos is for the most part lost; ΕΥΚΑΡΠΙΩΝΟΣ ΣΤΡΑΤ ΜΗΝΙ ΔΕΚΕΜΒΡ, 'of Eukarpion, soldier, month of December' (W).

ΑΝΑΝΙΟΥ ΠΡΕΣΒ ΜΗΝΙ ΙΑΝΟΥΑΡΙ, "of Ananias, presbyter, month of January". He stands together with a saint of which only the initial A has been preserved (NW).

23. Basiliskos' shoulder mark depicting two small human figures. Other shoulder marks show a single figure or geometrical patterns.

ΒΑΣΙΛΙΣΚΟΥ ΣΤΡΑ ΜΗΝΙ ΑΠΡΙΛΙΟΥ, "of Basiliskos, soldier, month of April"; ΠΡΙΣΚΟΥ ΣΤΡΑ ΜΗΝΙ ΟΚΤΩΒΡΙ, "of Priskos, soldier, month of October" (N).

23

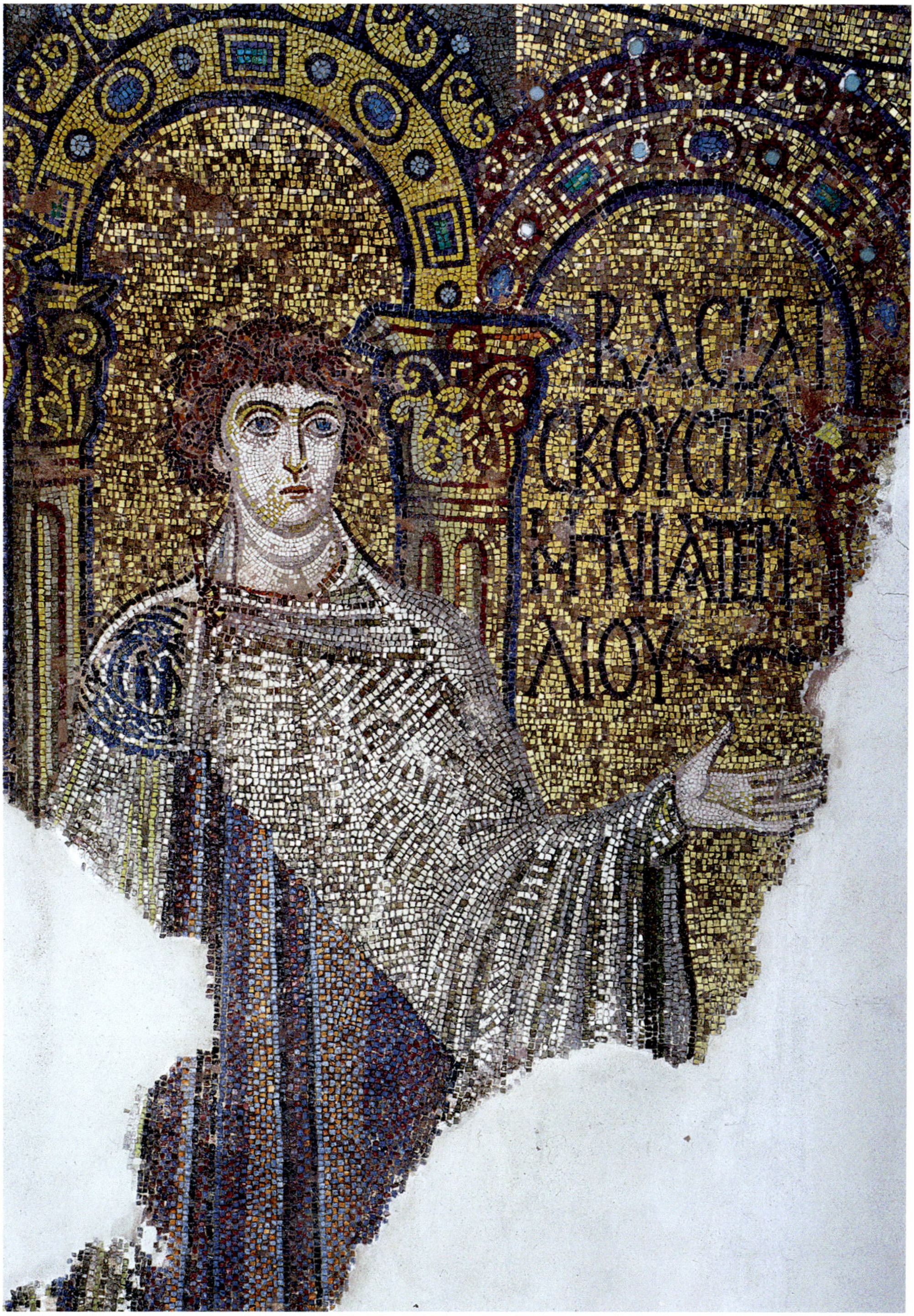

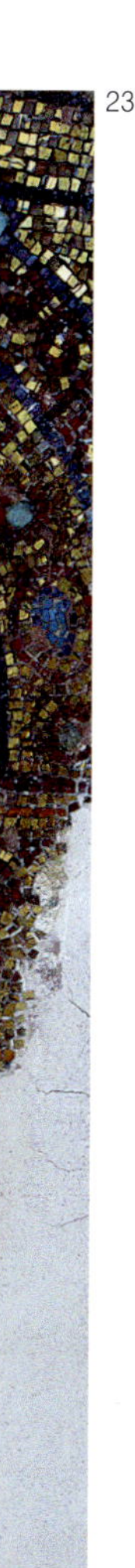

ΦΙΛΙΠΠΟΥ ΕΠΙΣΚ ΜΗΝΙ ΟΚΤΩΒΡ, "of Philippos, bishop, month of October"; ΘΕΡΙΝΟΥ ΣΤΡΑΤ ΜΗΝΙ ΙΟΥΛ, "of Therinos, soldier, month of July"; ΚΥΡΙΛ ΕΠΙΣΚ ΜΗΝΙ Ι, "of Kyrillos, bishop month of (June or July)" (NE).

The martyrs stand on a narrow strip of floor, or, rather than actually standing, they seem almost to float, an impression heightened by their proportionally small feet. The men are set off clearly from the surrounding architecture. The civilians (laymen and clerics) wear a *paenula*, a wide, circular-cut outer-garment that covers most of the body from the neck down [22]. The *paenulae* of the clerics (Ananias, Philippos and Kyrillos) are purple, while those of the laymen are either purple (Philemon, Porphyrios) or white (Kosmas, Damian and A...). Under the *paenula* the civilians wear a *dalmatica*, which is visible only at the hem and neckline. The colour of this is dark violet, except for Porphyrios, whose *dalmatica* in white contrasts with his purple *paenula*. As for the inner garment, the violet long-sleeved *tunica manicata*, only the cuffs are visible.

The soldiers are dressed in *chlamys* (cloak, mantle) [24]. Most of the soldier saints wear a white *chlamys* that was originally interspersed with glittering silver, now darkened. Leon (SE) and Eukarpion (W) are distinguished from the others by wearing imperial purple-violet cloaks [see 31, 45]. They are thus pictured as elect members of the imperial guard. All the soldiers' cloaks are fastened at the shoulder with a gold fibula. Under the cloak, one glimpses the short white tunic fastened with a golden-clasped belt, and under that, a long-sleeved inner tunic, also white. Both tunics are embellished with blue embroidery.

From the floor it is impossible to make out the marks of distinction on the shoulders of the soldiers' tunics. A close-up view, however, shows that while some have a geometrical decoration, others contain small motifs with either one (Onesiphoros, anonymous soldier) or two figures (Basiliskos) [23]. Despite the fact that such details were not visible from a distance, the artists took great pains to make each and every part of the saints and their attire as beautiful and perfect as possible. A parallel to the

24. Anonymous soldier martyr. He wears a white chlamys (cloak) originally interspersed with glittering silver. The chlamys is fastened at the shoulder with a gold fibula (pin).

24

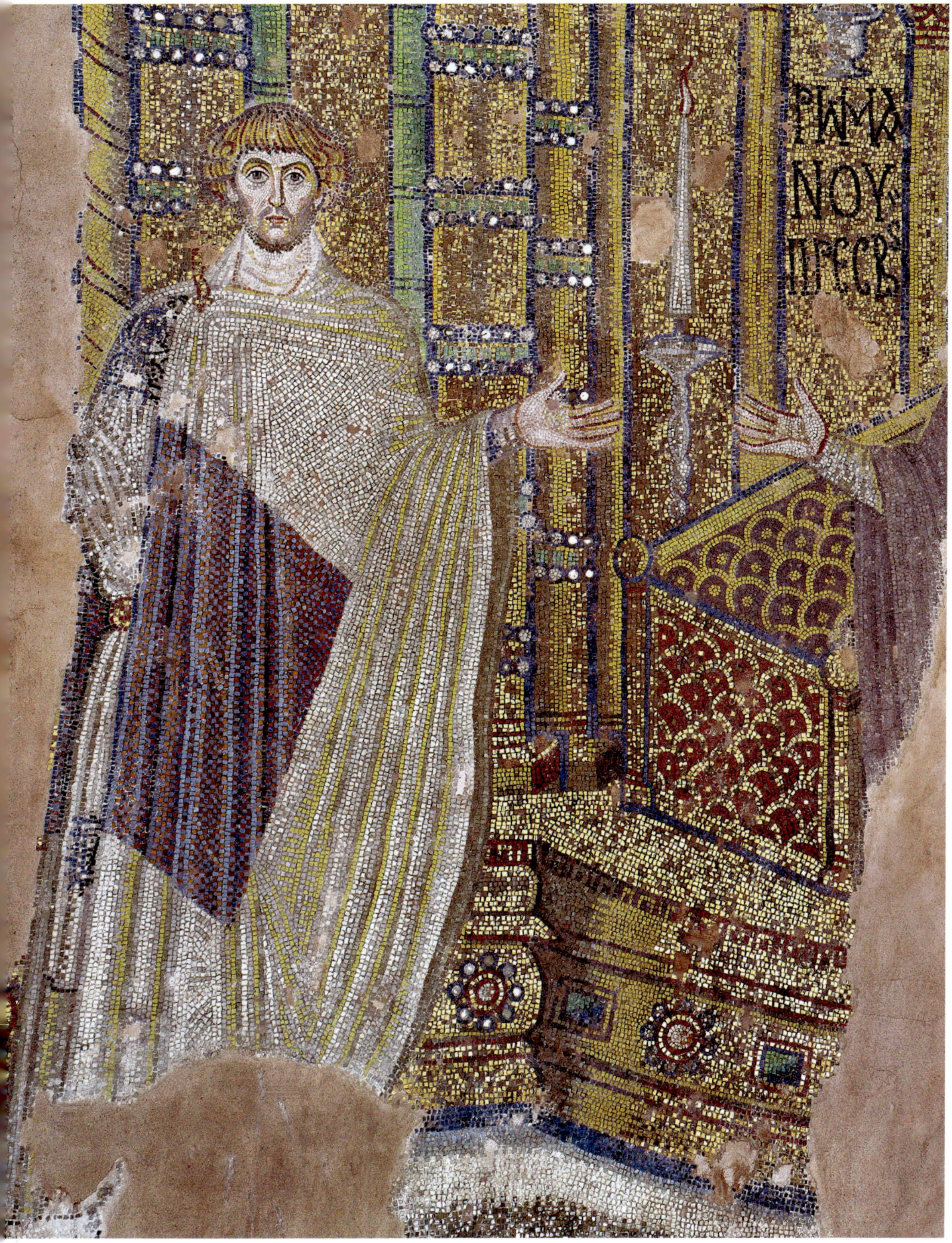

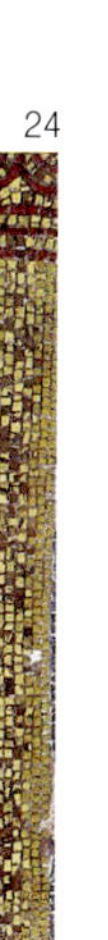

25

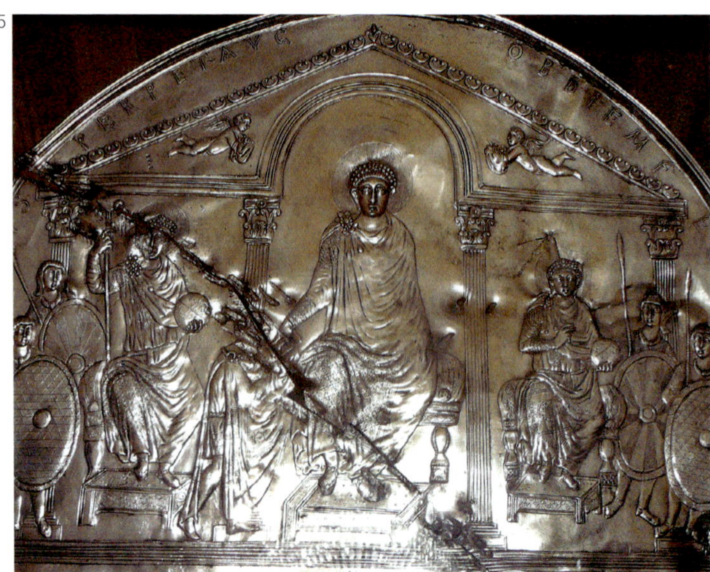

meticulous rendering of garments is the representations on the *missorium* of Theodosius, a large gilded silver plate issued on the occasion of the emperor's ten year anniversary celebrated in Thessaloniki in 388 (Madrid, Real Academia de la Historia). On this plate, the fibulae, insignia and intricately woven or embroidered patterns on the clothing of emperors and guards are meticulously rendered [25]. Clothes play an important role in visualizing status, and the saints in the heavenly court follow the fashions of the earthly court.

THE MARTYR PORTRAITS

The saints' faces reflect the undisturbed dignity of holy men. Their represented age ranges from the youth Priskos [26] to the old bishop Philippos [27]. As for hair, Leon, Philemon, Onesiphoros, Porphyrios, Basiliskos and Therinos have curly locks, while Priskos wears his hair straight; most soldiers are beardless, but the anonymous soldier and Therinos sport a moustache and slight beard growth. The mature martyrs, Kosmas and Damian, Ananias and A..., Philippos and Kyrillos, are bearded. The grooming of hair and beard is used to characterize the individual saints: The bishops Kyrillos and the balding Philippos have very long and full beards,

26

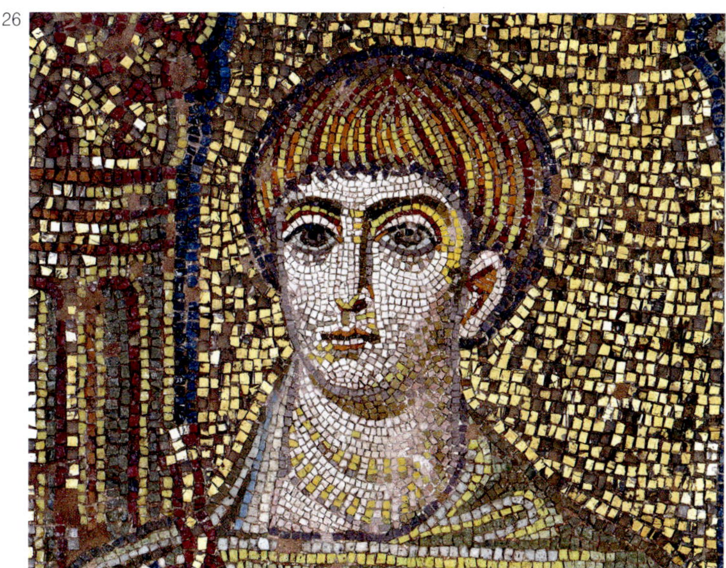

27

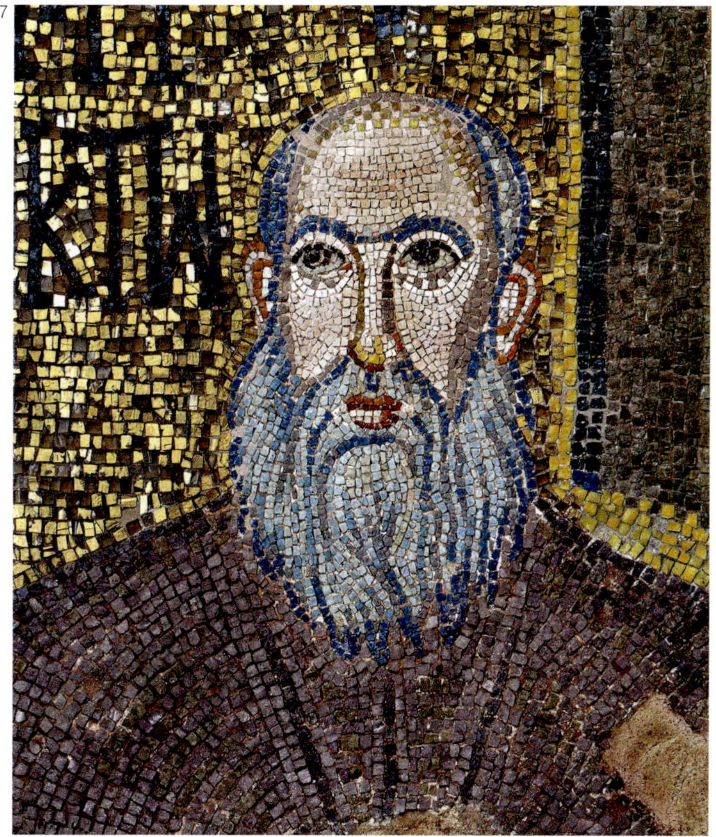

25. Theodosius' silver missorium, 388, enthroned emperors with bodyguards. Clothes and insignia are rendered in detail (Madrid, Real Academia de la Historia).

26. Portrait of the young soldier martyr Priskos.

27. Portrait of the old bishop martyr Philippos with long bluish beard and balding head.

28. Portrait of Alexander the Great (Copenhagen, Ny Carlsberg Glyptotek).

29. Portrait of the soldier martyr Onesiphoros with large mane of luxurious hair in the style of Alexander the Great.

while that of the presbyter Ananias is short. Damianos has a long forked beard characteristic of philosophers depicted on late antique floor mosaics. The saints thus present a varied portrait gallery.

The physician brothers Kosmas and Damianos (SW) stand on small plinths, a distinguishing feature. The emperor Theodosius' miraculous recovery from serious illness in Thessaloniki in 380 may have prompted the inclusion of the physician saints in the pictorial programme. These are presumably the earliest preserved images of the brothers. While most of the martyrs depicted in the Rotunda have long since lapsed into oblivion, Kosmas and Damianos remained popular throughout the Middle Ages, and their imagery is therefore of special interest. Both have long beards: that of Kosmas is silvery blue-grey, while that of Damianos is a darker purplish-blue.

The soldier Onesiphoros [29] and his companion, the civilian Porphyrios, are depicted as handsome youths in idealized guise with full manes of curly locks and fine faces. Onesiphoros' "lion's mane", firm chin and large eyes call to mind idealized posthumous images of Alexander the Great [28]. Portraits of Alexander were preserved in late antiquity, and epigraphical evidence in the form of inscribed statue bases shows that new images of the Macedonian king were set up in Thessaloniki at least as late as the third century AD. Alexander's official portraiture symbolized his *ethos*, his upright character, and embodied both physical and spiritual strength, so he was a fitting model for a young soldier martyr.

28

In search of a model for such mature and aging saints as the bishops Philippos and Kyrillos, the mosaicists and their advisors could turn to images of philosophers. This was a popular theme for both floors and sculpted images in late antiquity. Philippos' distinctive physiognomy, with large, balding head, drooping moustache and long, slightly ragged beard, is particularly close to some late antique images of Socrates. By late antiquity the mature to elderly bearded head —whether it was intended to stand for a philosopher, a poet or a sage— had be-

29

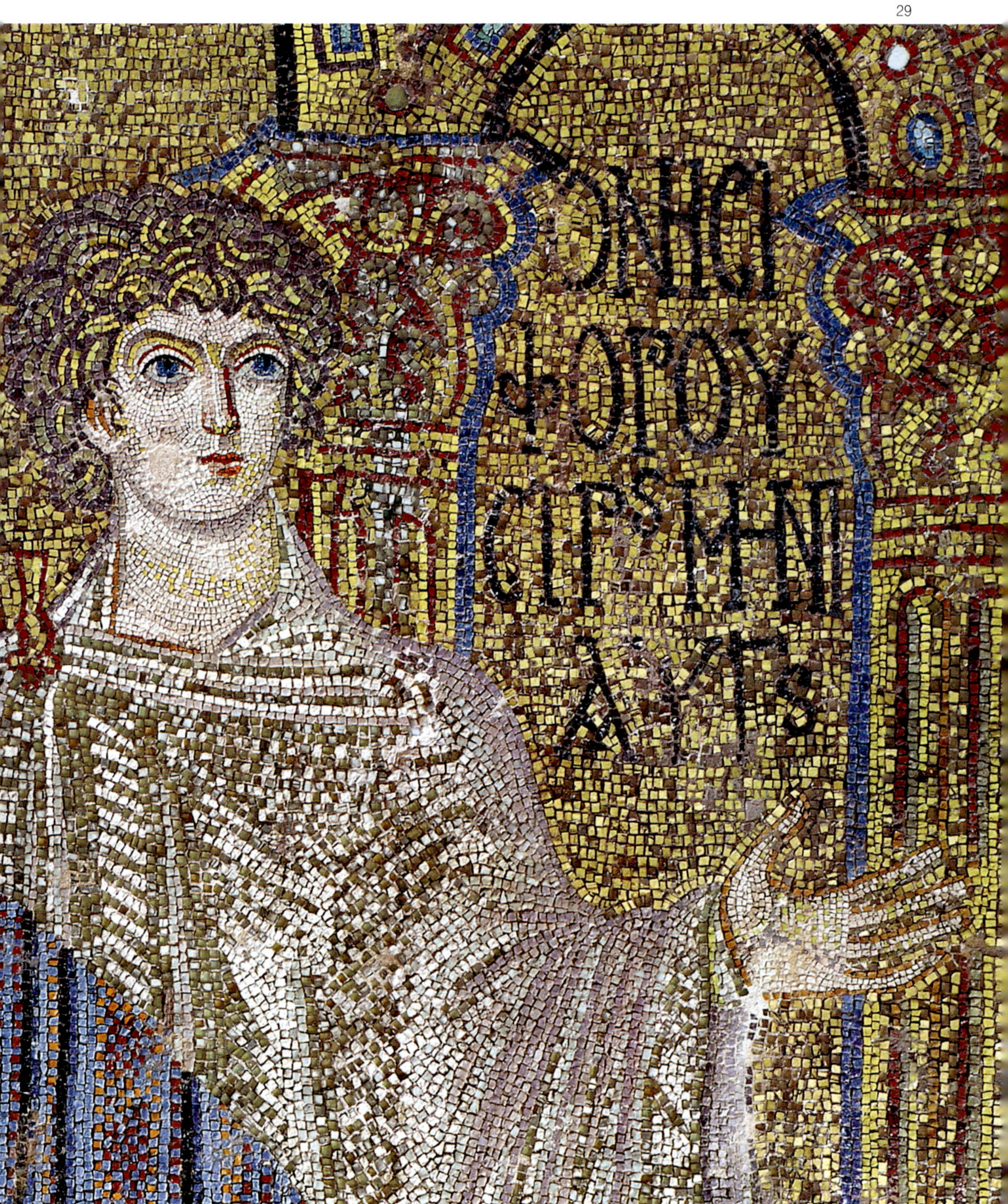

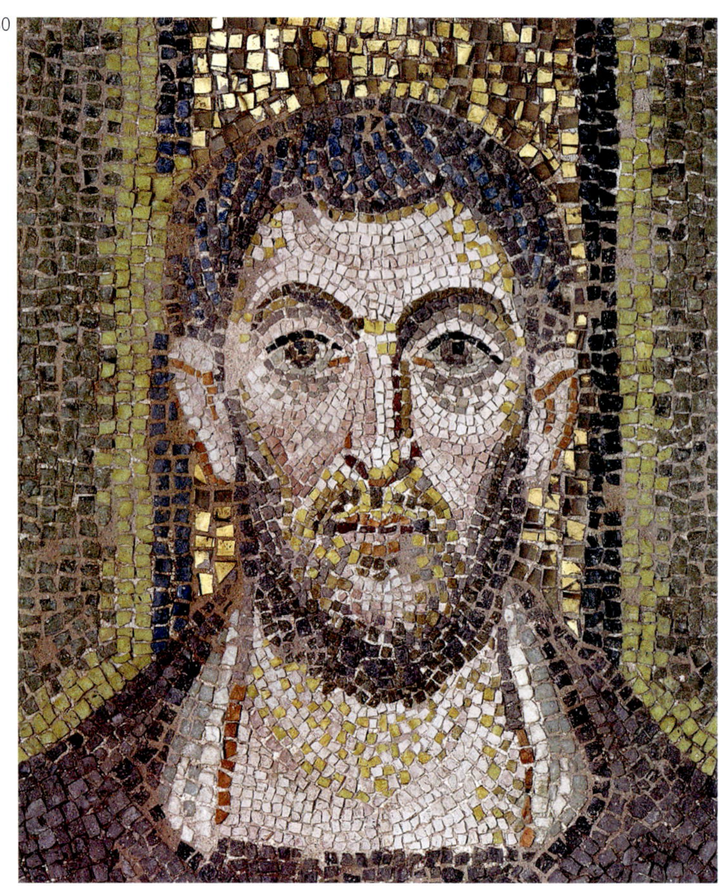

come a general symbol of *sophia* that could be used to portray Christians as well as pagans.

Good parallels to most of the saints can be found in art of the second to fourth centuries. The mummy portraits from Fayum in Egypt, which are preserved due to favourable climatic conditions, furnish many examples. Among these portraits, one can find heads that look quite like the physiognomies of Therinos and Ananias [30]. Indeed, the saints' portraits are firmly situated in the antique tradition. This conservatism is unsurprising when considering that these mosaics (if the date in the reign of Theodosius I is correct) must be among the earliest representations of martyrs. No *schemata* or formulas for representing individual saints or classes of saints had yet been established.

30. Portrait of the ecclesiastic martyr Ananias. His hair and short beard are set in shades of violet and dark blue.

In the Rotunda, the holy men are depicted in a manner that stresses their individuality, no two saints being alike. The faces are set with smaller tesserae than the rest of the mosaics. The heads were made by specialists in a workshop and subsequently inserted into bodies finished *in situ* in the cupola. This approach differs from the normal procedure of setting mosaic tesserae directly into the wall (see the section on technique). We can therefore speculate whether some of the representations were based on a true portrait tradition. A portrait of a martyr could originate from a commemorative image made for the martyr's tomb. Such images could then have been copied and distributed on amulets or small portable icons. Nevertheless, whether the portraits are factual (derived from a portrait tradition based on the martyr's physical appearance) or fictitious (derived from antique generalized types), the differentiation and individualization of the heads prove that the artists intended to distinguish each saint from his companion.

MARTYRS AND RELICS

As we have seen, each inscription gives a name, profession and festal month [31]. But the order in which the months are presented does not follow the calendar year, and the day of the month on which the saint was commemorated is not given. The presentation of the martyrs is therefore not intended primarily as a liturgical calendar. Rather, the recording of each saint's month of commemoration serves to make sure that the martyr in question is properly identified. Another characteristic of the inscriptions is that the names are given in the genitive case, e.g., *Leontos*, where one might have expected the name in the nominative case, *Leon*. So the intended meaning must be that the image stands for some particular aspect of the saint, such as his image, soul, commemoration day, testimony, or perhaps relics.

Relics were deposed under the altar of the church, and earlier excavations have documented the existence of two subterranean crypts to the east and west of the Rotunda. They most probably were used for burying martyr relics. It is probable that relics or *brandea* (contact relics) of all the twenty saints that were originally represented in the mosaics were kept in the church or in the exterior crypts.

Most of the martyrs were identified from hagiographical sources already in the nineteenth century (Texier in 1864). Except for Onesiphoros and Porphyrios, who were contemporaries of Saint Paul, most of the martyrs were executed around 300 in the persecutions of Diocletian. Philippos [27] is probably identical to Philippos from Thrakia, who was decapitated as an old man in Hadrianopolis in 303, while his companion Kyrillos has been identified with the martyr of that name who became bishop around 280 at the age of 70 and was decapitated at Gortyn in Crete in 304. The martyr Leon [31] is shown as a young man with golden locks (arranged in a hairstyle that was in fashion during Theodosius' reign, as seen in the reliefs on the obelisk base in Constantinople, 390). He may be identical to a soldier who was executed in the reign of the Arian emperor Constantius II, as late as around 350. The visual manifestations of the martyrs therefore seem to be in keeping with the evidence of their *vitae*. (This does not necessarily imply that the martyrs actually looked like their portraits, since the portraits may have been designed to fit the general image of, respectively, a very old or a very young man).

The hagiographical evidence indicates that the martyrs who can be identified lived in the Eastern Empire. There is no indication that martyrs from the Western Empire —or female martyrs— were among the lost figures. It is reasonable to assume that the holy men, including the lost figures, were selected in order to represent all the East Roman administrative dioceses, that is, the dioceses in Theodosius' part of the Empire. They therefore also function as symbolic representations of the territories.

Martyrs served a special role as protectors. Shortly before the year 400, John Chrysostomos writes about the martyrs in Antioch or Constantinople, that their tombs surround the city like a protective wall (*De martyres Aegyptos* 1; Patrologia Graeca 50, 694). The priests and laymen and, in particular,

31. Martyr Leon with inscription giving name, profession and festal month ΛΕΟΝΤΟΣ ΣΤΡΑΤ ΜΗΝΙ ΙΟΥΝ, Leon, soldier, June.

31

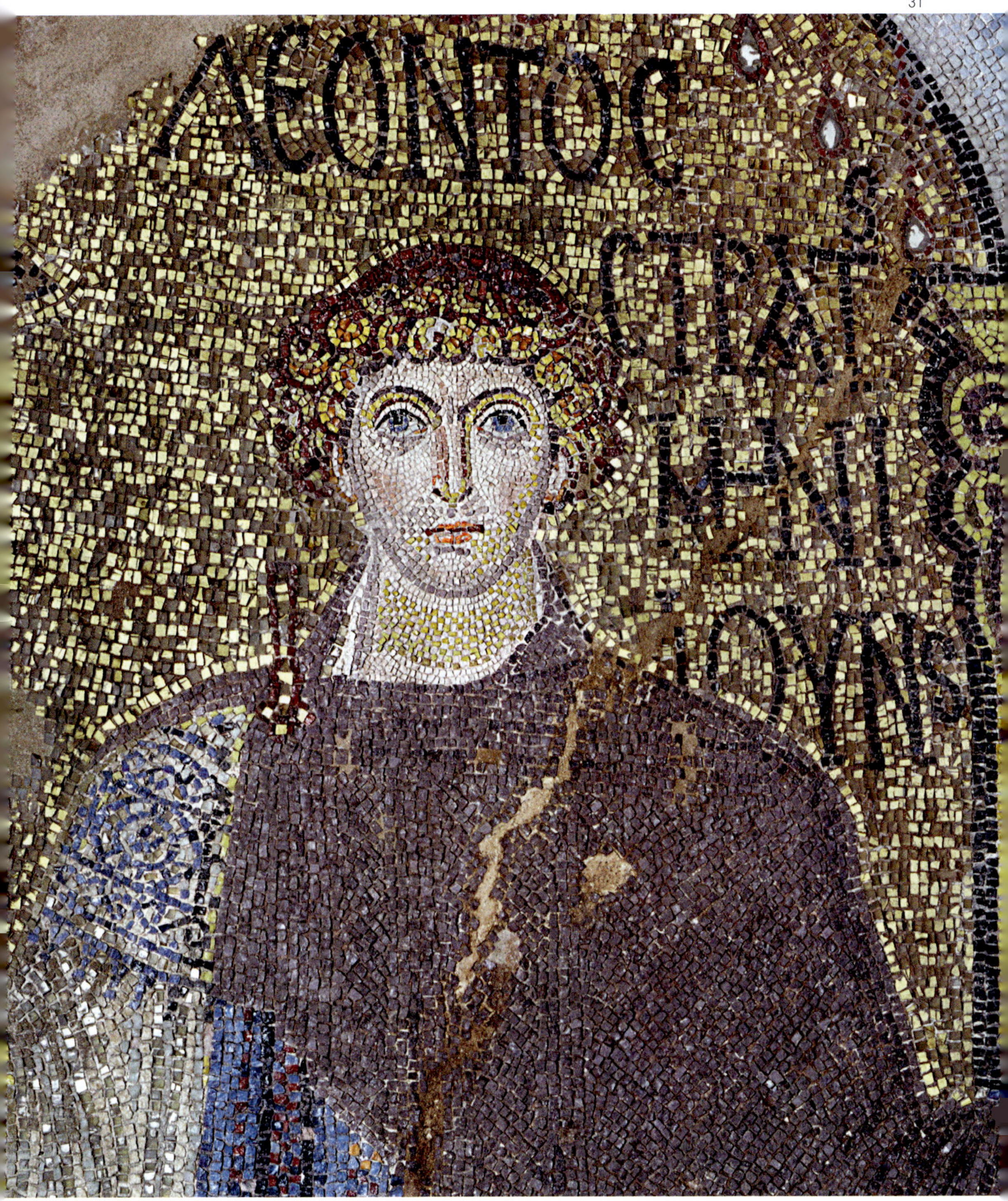

32

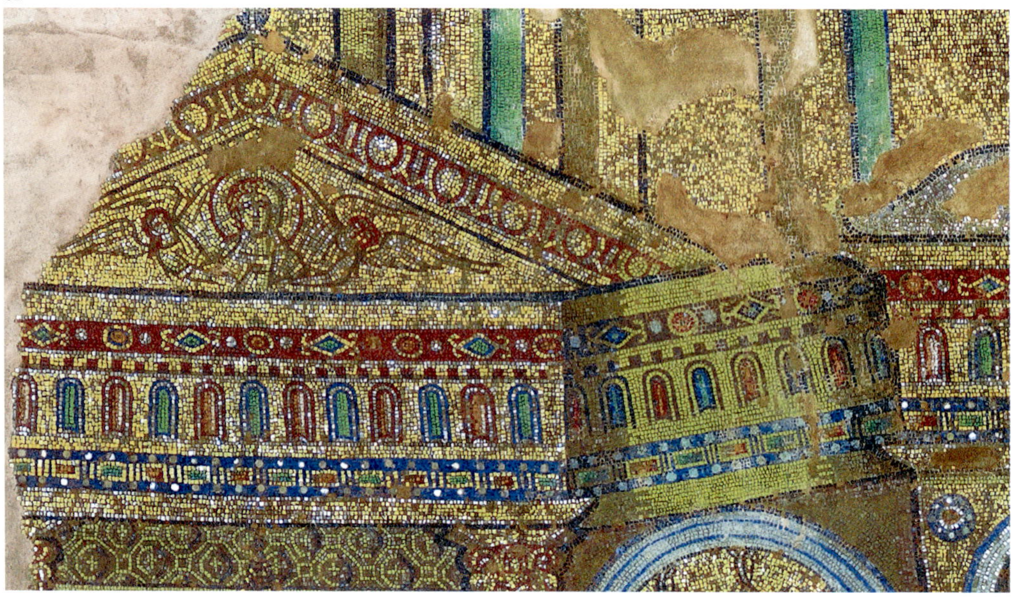

32. Small pediment above the soldier martyr Therinos, showing the nimbed bust of Christ supported by two flying angels.

the many soldier saints in the Rotunda can similarly be said to function like divine protectors; depicted in the mosaics and thus present in effigy, and presumably also present in relics, they encircle and guard the emperor and his realm.

The two panels on either side of the choir both contain three martyrs. In the centre of one panel (SE) is the soldier Leon, flanked by a no-longer extant saint and by Philemon; in the centre of the other panel (NE) is the soldier Therinos, flanked by the old bishops. The two soldiers are singled out by the crown suspended above their heads, and —still preserved in Therinos' panel— by a pediment depicting a bust of Christ supported by two angels [32]. This image, familiar from sarcophagus reliefs, is a shorthand version of the iconography in the Rotunda's central medallion. Placed in close proximity to the choir's entrance, these saints guard the high altar of the church.

DOGMATIC THEMES IN THE MARTYR ZONE

The holy martyrs inhabit the golden structures that visualize the heavenly Jerusalem, but even more messages are contained within the intricate iconography of the mosaics. Some martyrs serve an additional function either as witnesses to or as part of complex images of dogmatic signification. Three dogmatic themes, each depicted twice (including the lost east panel), are presented in the architectural imagery [34–36]. The first theme, flanked by Onesiphoros and Porphyrios (S), and by Basiliskos and Priskos (N), consists of a large jewelled cross crowned by a dove and placed in front of a basin of water. The second theme, flanked by Kosmas and Damianos (SW), and by A... and Ananias (NW), is a codex displayed on a finely adorned chair placed on top of a stepped podium. The third theme is represented by the (all but lost) priest Romanos standing in prayer in front of a choir screen (W). A corresponding theme originally was seen in the lost panel over the choir to the east. The sacred character of the three themes is underlined by pairs of flanking candelabra with burning candles, and by their placement either in front of a magnificent ciborium (themes 1, 2) or in a vaulted exedra (theme 3).

The first theme —dove, cross, basin— refers to baptism and thereby to the Holy Trinity. The glorification of the dove in the Trinitarian motif may be understood as the Orthodox emperor Theodosius' challenge to the Arian *pneumatomachoi*, "spirit-fighters", who denied the full godhead of the Holy Spirit. The cross symbolizes Christ, while the water of baptism invokes the invisible Father, whose voice from heaven said: "This is my beloved son" (Matthew 3.17). The codex in the second theme is the Gospel book, the words of Christ. In the third theme, the choir and the officiating priest symbolize the Heavenly Church that emanates from the teaching of Christ and the twelve apostles. The imagery thus stands for the celestial confirmation of the creed formulated at Nicaea in 325 in the presence of the emperor Constantine the Great: The Orthodox dogma of the Trinity (theme 1) is based on the teaching of Christ (theme 2) and confirmed in the liturgy of the Heavenly Church (theme 3). More specifically, these images can be understood as a visualization of the Christian creed formulated in Theodosius' edict *Cunctos populi*, "to all people". This edict was promulgated from the

33. Reconstruction of dogmatic theme: Trinity.

34–36. Dogmatic themes: Trinity (1), Codex (2), Heavenly Church (3) (H. Torp).

imperial palace at Thessaloniki on 28 February 380. The edict set forth the defining criteria of orthodoxy: "according to the *apostolic discipline* and the *evangelic doctrine*, we shall believe in the single Deity of the Father, the Son and the Holy Spirit, under the concept of equal majesty and of the *Holy Trinity*". The Rotunda mosaics therefore give visual form to the religious-political message which Theodosius directed against the Arians.

The exaltation of the Holy Spirit, situated in the palatine

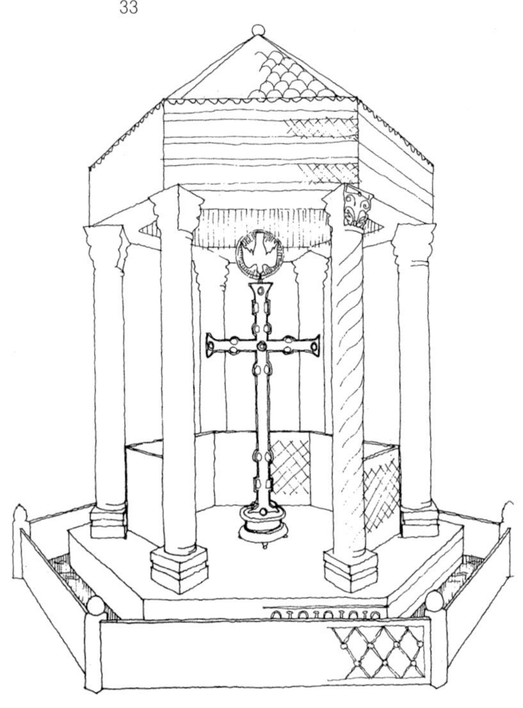

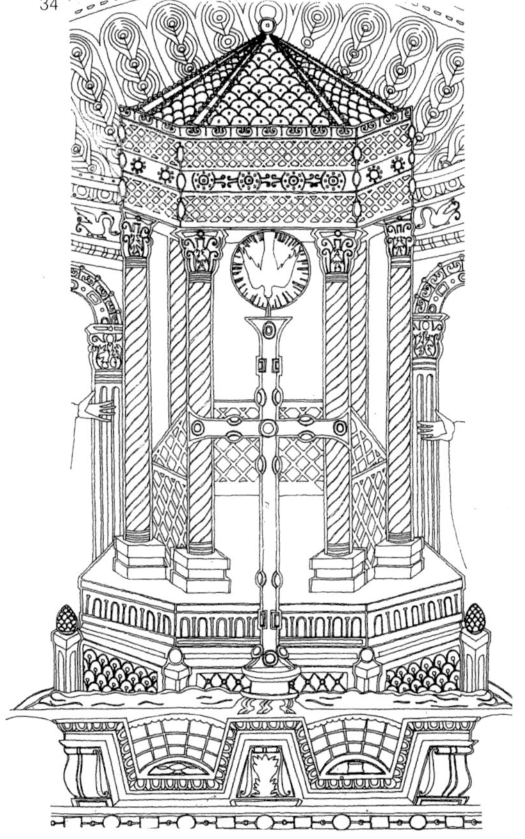

north-south axis of the church, is clearly the fundamental message of the dogmatic themes. In fact, one of the main reasons for Theodosius' prolonged stay in Thessaloniki may have been the Arians', and especially, the *pneumatomachoi's* hold on Constantinople. In addition to serving as Theodosius' palace church during his sojourn in Thessaloniki, the Rotunda may therefore be understood as a monument to his Trinitarian faith, as defined in the imperial Edict of 380.

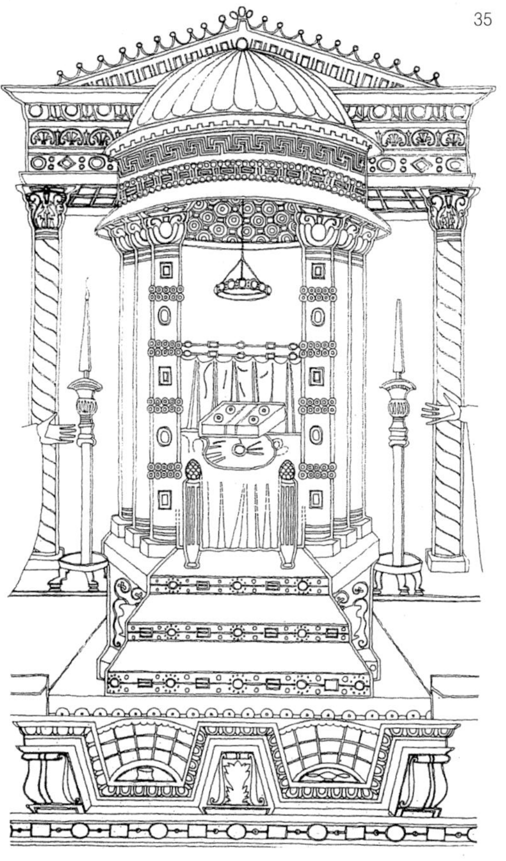

35

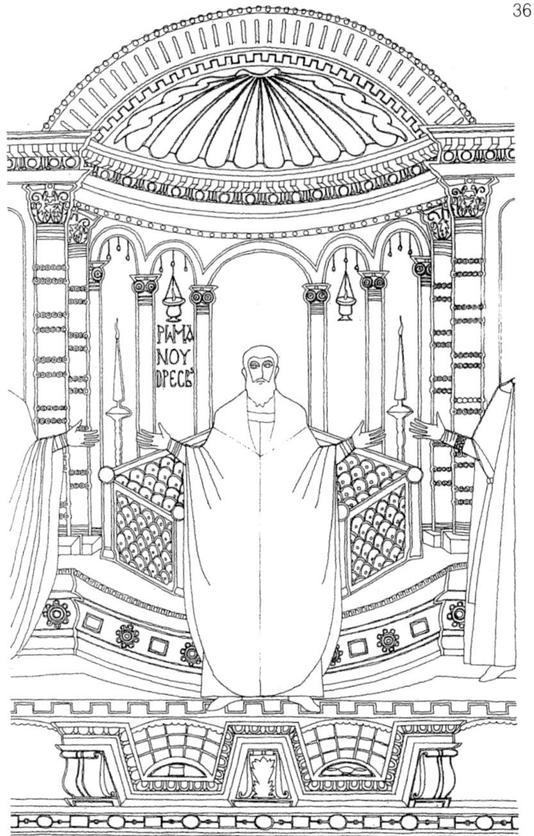

36

37. Preliminary sketch of Christ in medallion (S. Sass).

38. Medallion in the cupola's zenith with Christ supported by flying angels. The preliminary sketch is painted in black directly on the brickwork. Of Christ remains in mosaic the raised right hand, part of the nimbus and the top of the long cross-staff.

39. Bands of silver stars, a garland of flowers and fruit, and a rainbow encircling the medallion. Heavy-faced angel supporting the medallion.

The Medallion of Christ Supported by Flying Angels

The mosaic medallion in the cupola's zenith is situated about 28 metres above the current floor level. The medallion's east-west diameter measures 7.35 metres [38]. Most of the mosaic is lost and it is difficult at first to see what was represented. Looking closely, however, one will be able to make out a sketch painted in black directly on the brickwork [38]. It shows an about 4 metre-tall, full-figure Christ in striding motion. His raised right hand, the upper part of the golden nimbus and the top of a long golden cross-staff are still extant in mosaic. Slight remains of the

37

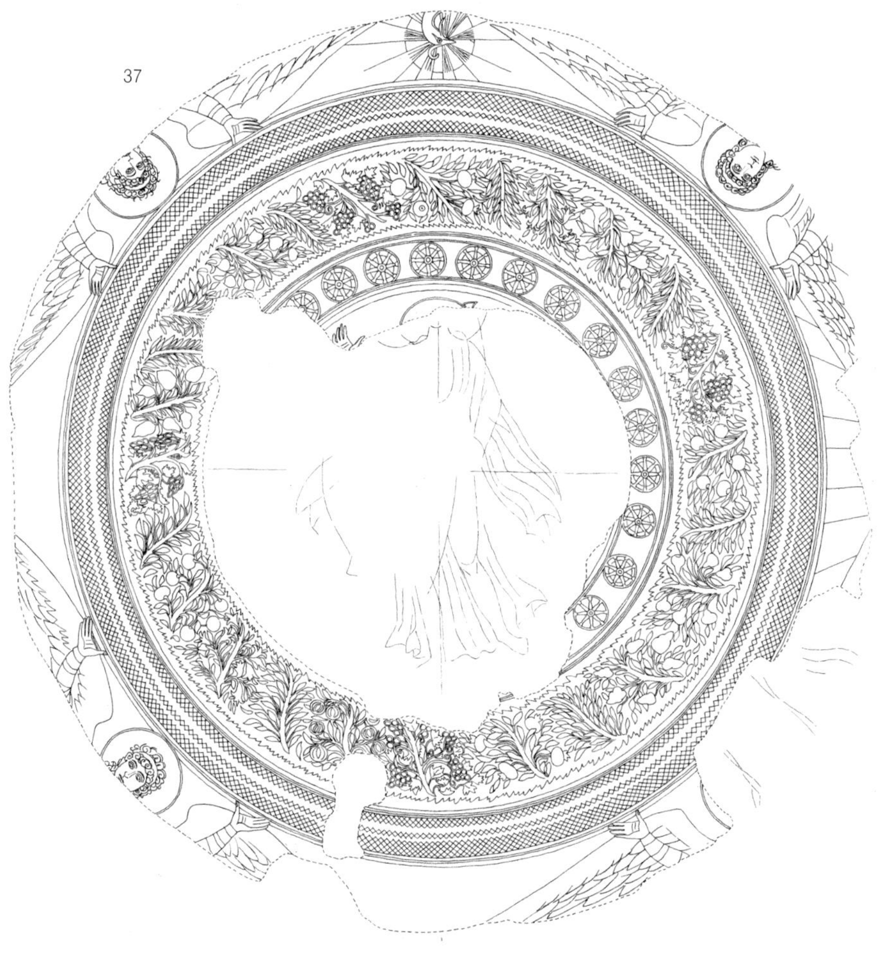

38

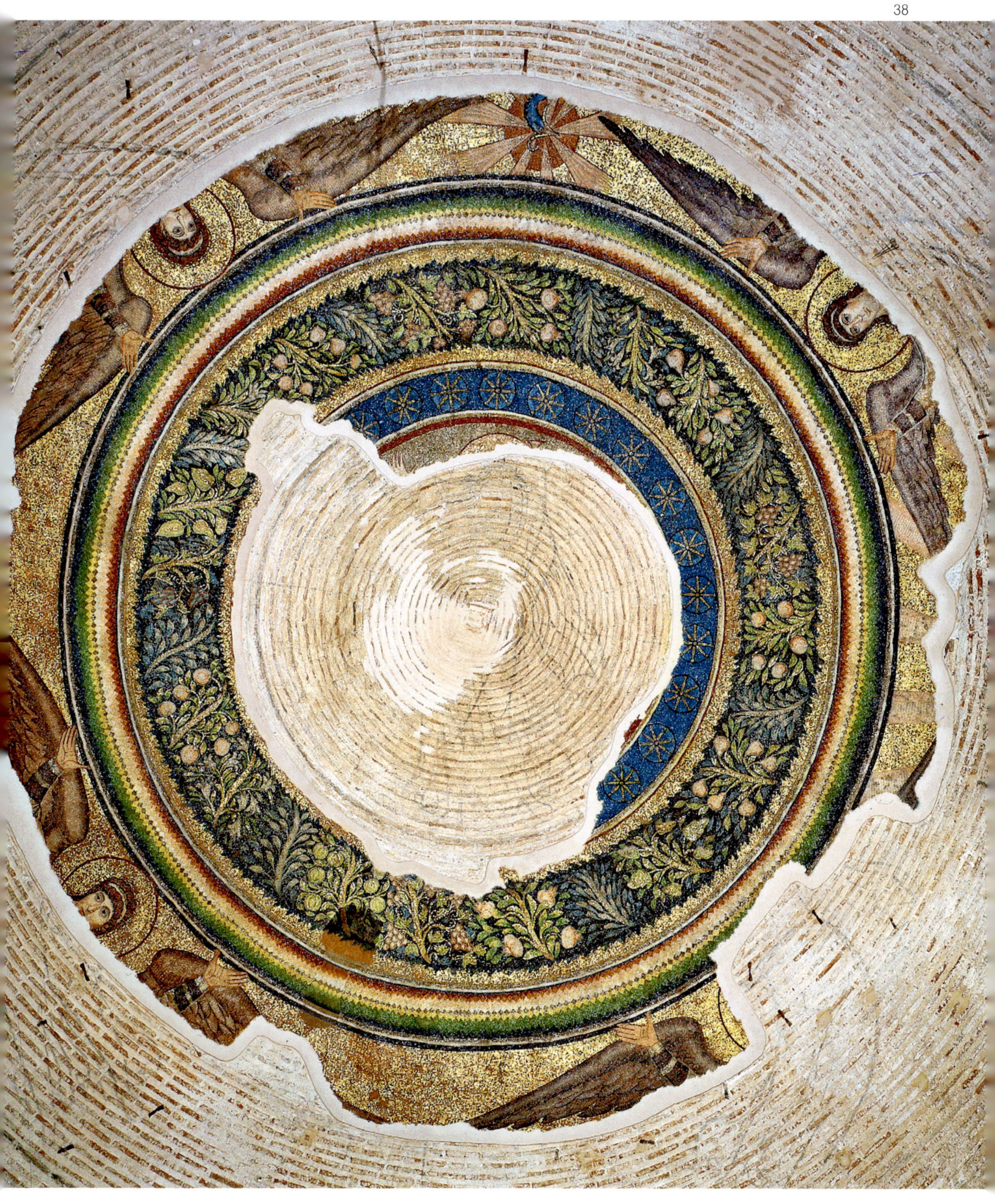

39

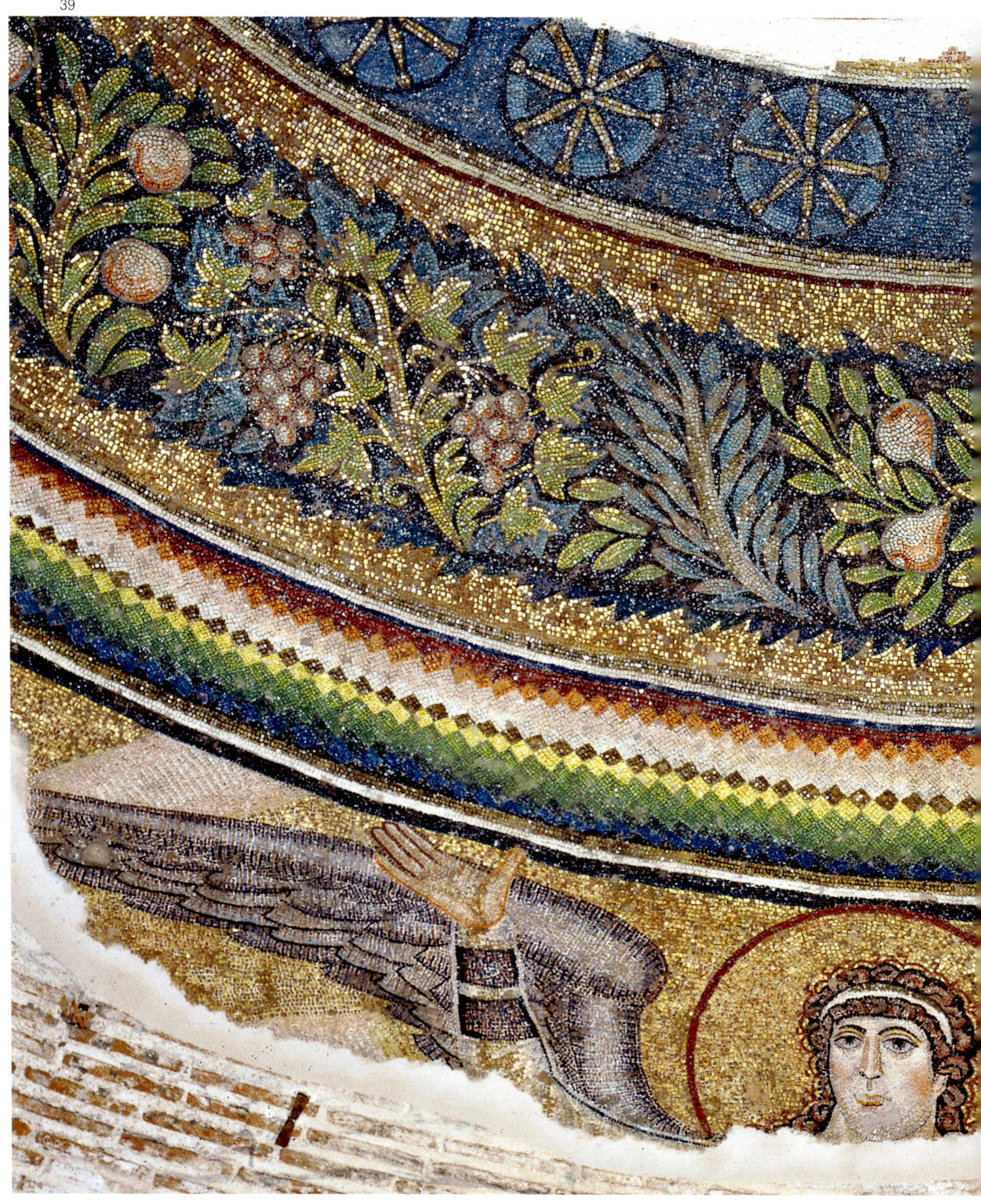

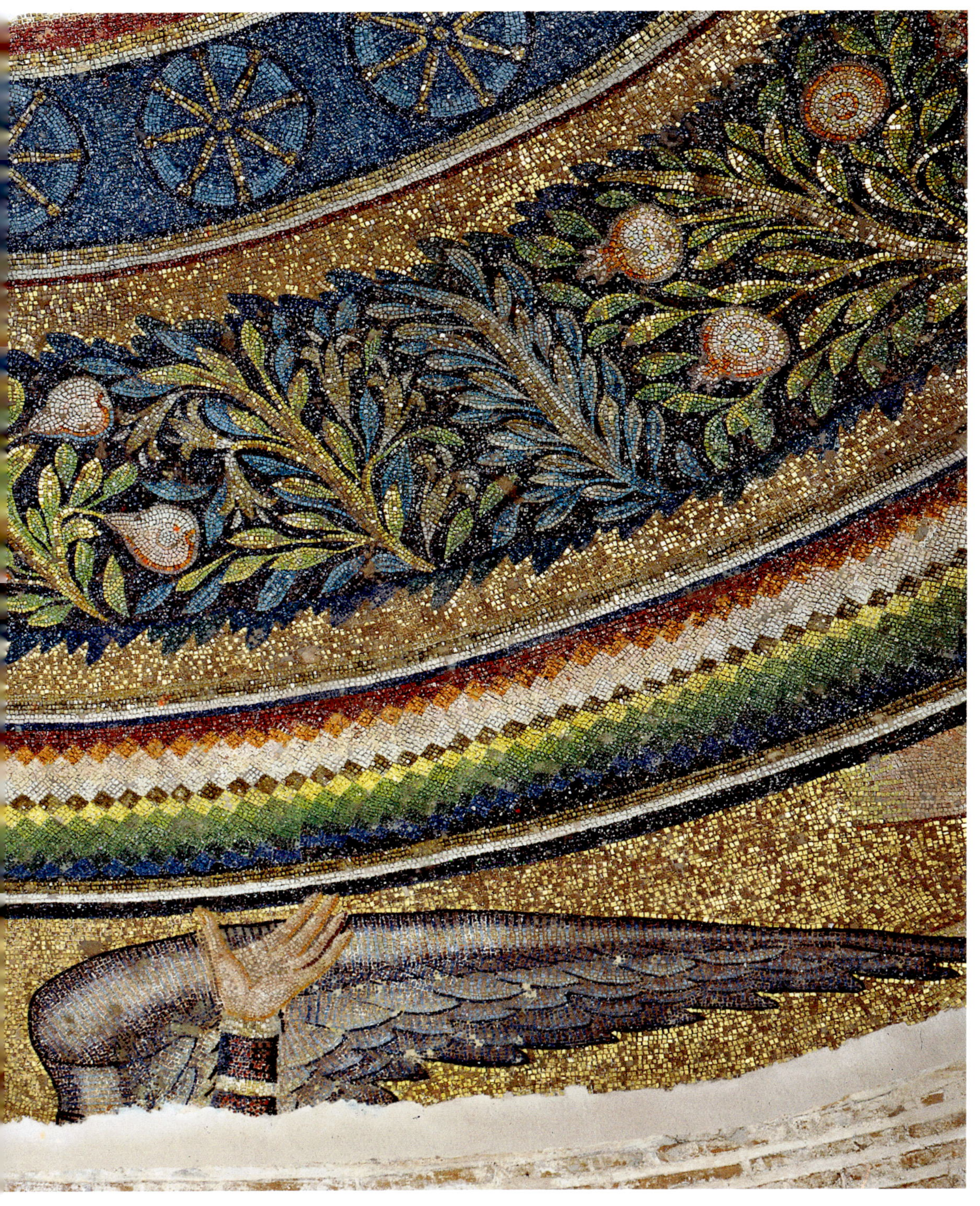

silver ground are also preserved. The sketch shows that Christ is wearing a wide, full-length chiton and a billowing *chlamys* (cloak, mantle). It is worth noting that this is not the philosopher's tunic and pallium usually worn by Christ (and the angels), but the ideal costume of Apollo-Sol-Helios. In 330, Constantine the Great erected a colossal statue in gilded bronze of Constantine-Helios on top of a porphyry column in his forum in Constantinople. This statue probably influenced the representation of this particular type of Christ in the Rotunda mosaics. The raised right hand is the characteristic gesture of power and the gesture of the personification of *Sol Invictus*, the invincible sun. Taken together, the raised right hand and the garments indicate a solar interpretation of the Rotunda Christ: *Christus Lux Mundi*, Christ the light of the world.

One must imagine a radiant Christ-Sol advancing through shimmering silvery light, further illuminated by a blaze of light from the stars and the rainbow that surround him. The three concentric bands that frame the divine image consist of silver stars on a blue ground, a garland of fruit and flowers and, in the outer circle, a rainbow, a symbol of divine presence (Ezekiel 1.28). The circle of silver stars, originally counting twenty-eight, suggests the light of the night, while the coloured light of the rainbow represents daylight [39].

The Phoenix, the fire-bird, just east of Christ's head, and the rays of light emanating from the no-longer-extant cross, to the west, both underscore the light symbolism [40]. Eternity and rebirth are stressed by the presence of Phoenix. This is also the theme of the large evergreen wreath: it is made of twenty-five sections of branches with white lilies, laurel, vines and various fruit, such as pears, grapes and pomegranates, all set in regularly repeated sections. By displaying plants associated with all the four seasons, the wreath symbolizes renewal, resurrection and eternity.

40. The head of the Phoenix, the fire-bird, with rays of light.

41. Sweet-faced angel. The angel's garment was white embellished with purple bands.

The cosmic medallion is supported by four hovering angels, who, with their fingertips, barely touch the edge of the rainbow. They are only partly preserved, but one can follow the outlines of

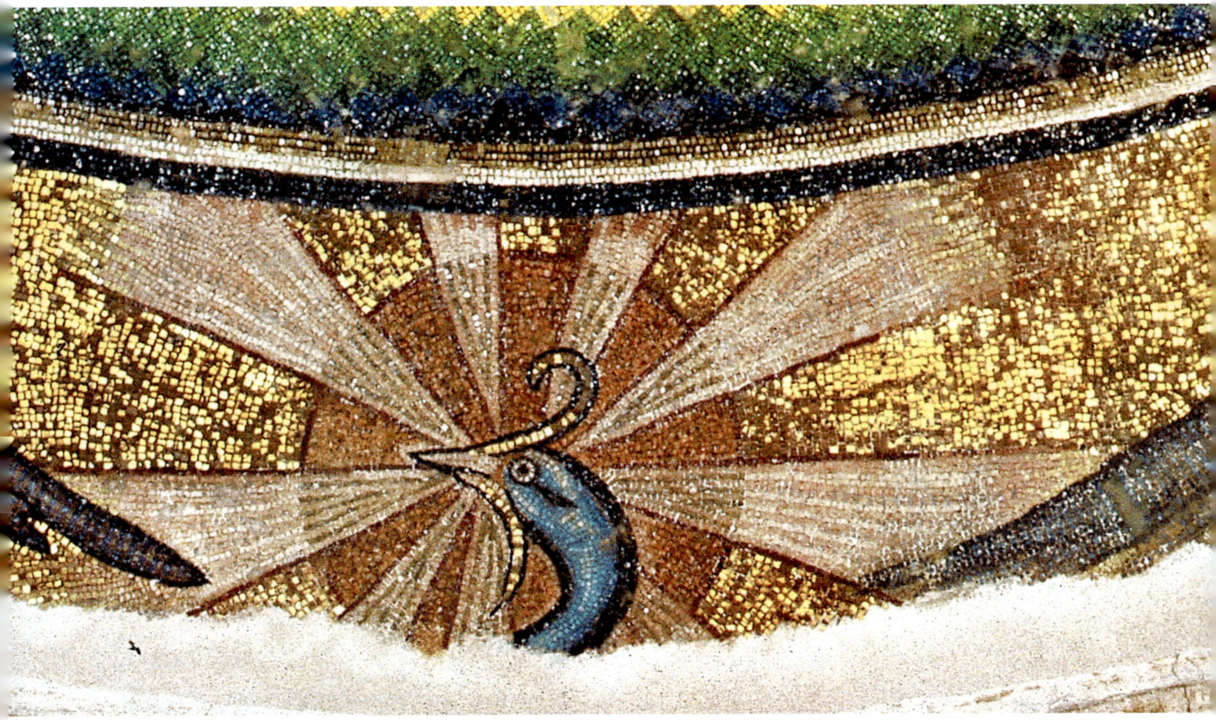

41

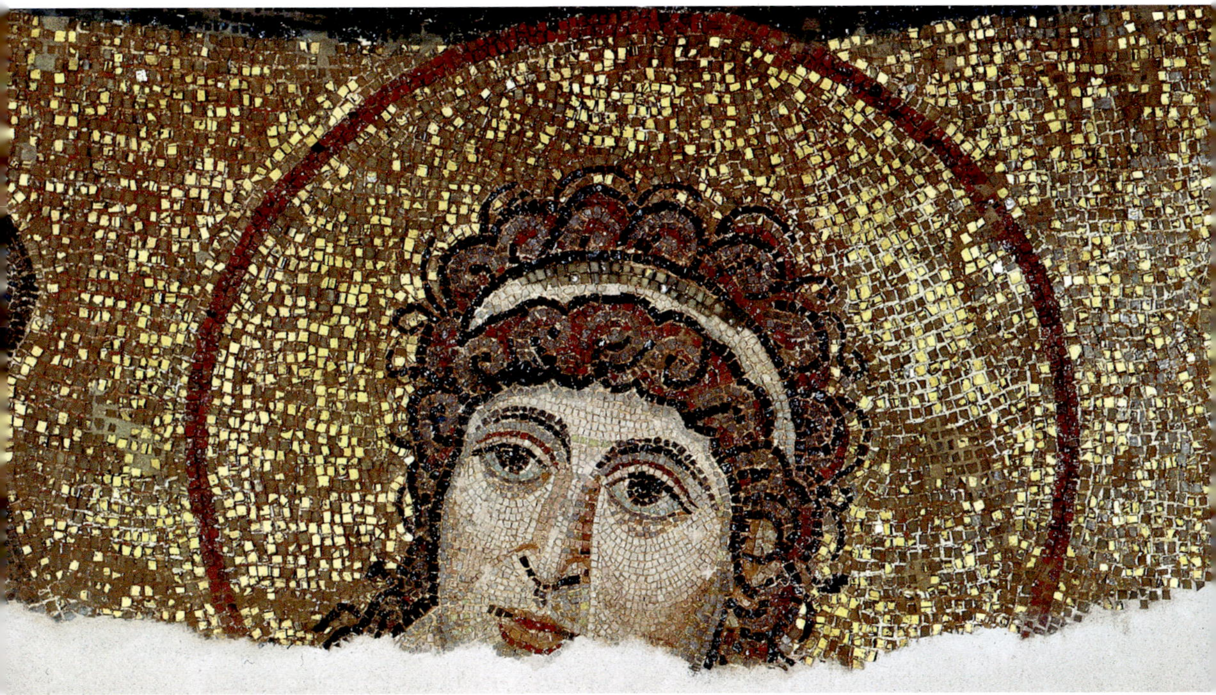

their flowing garments painted in black on the brickwork. What remains are the purple and silver cuffs of their long-sleeved white tunicae. Two angels have fine physiognomies: they appear as beautiful, almost feminine youths. Their curly hair is rendered in shades of red and their facial features are delicate [41]. But the mosaicists made distinctions even between angels, as the third angel, to the north-east, shows a totally different, heavier and masculine physiognomy [39]. This distinctive physiognomy brings to mind portraits of Constantinian emperors, such as the large bronze head in the Capitoline museum in Rome, a portrait of either Constantine or one of his sons. It is likely that the fourth angel, to the north-west, whose head unfortunately is lost, also had heavy facial features.

Looking up at the cupola from the floor, one senses that the angels are in gentle motion. From tip to tip, the wing span of the angels reaches an impressive 5 metres. The wings are designed in fine colour gradations that further underscore their lightness and airiness. The heavy-faced angels in the northern part of the sphere have darker wings than do their companions in the southern part. The feathers of all angels are set with various tones of blue, ranging from greyish blue to ultramarine, in addition to violet and red. Impressionistic or optical colour blending in blue and red was used to give an impression of lightly fluttering feathers. Tesserae in lighter tones suggest highlights. Under optimal lightning conditions, it would have appeared as though light was striking their shimmering feathers. The non-naturalistic blending sustained the angels' quality of being *asomatoi*, bodiless, weightless beings.

The visual subtleties of the mosaics will be further discussed in the section on aesthetic aspects. But before turning to aesthetics, a few words about the mosaic technique are pertinent, since the material and the setting technique also define the mosaic style.

The Mosaic Technique

Originally, the cupola mosaics covered about 900 square metres. To create them, millions of tiny mosaic cubes (tesserae) were required [42]. As is characteristic for Byzantine mosaics in general, the Rotunda tesserae are not set strictly in plain with the ground but are somewhat irregularly inclined. Pieces of different sizes and shapes, when inserted at varying angles, make the surface vibrate with light as it reflects from the many angles. Some tesserae are cut in limestone or marble, but most consist of glass. The tesserae of gold- and silver-glass are made by sandwiching a very thin gold or silver foil between two layers of glass. For coloured glass, the artists included a large range of hues such as yellow, orange, red, purple, violet, blue, turquoise and green. Each hue encompasses many shades, thus the blues, for instance, range from the palest light blue to the darkest, almost black ultramarine; other blues are greenish or turquoise. It seems impossible to count the number of hues because one shade turns imperceptibly into the next. The impression of colour variation also depends on lightning conditions and each viewer's subjective visual perception. Where one person may distinguish two colour gradations, another may perceive three, four or five.

42. Setting technique of gold and glass tesserae. Pieces of different sizes and shapes are inserted at varying angles.

43. Detail of mosaic technique, eastern light opening: vegetal decoration.

42

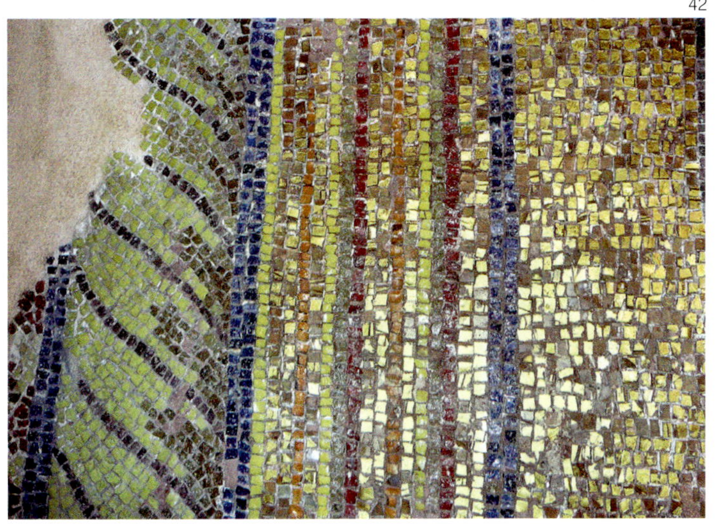

43

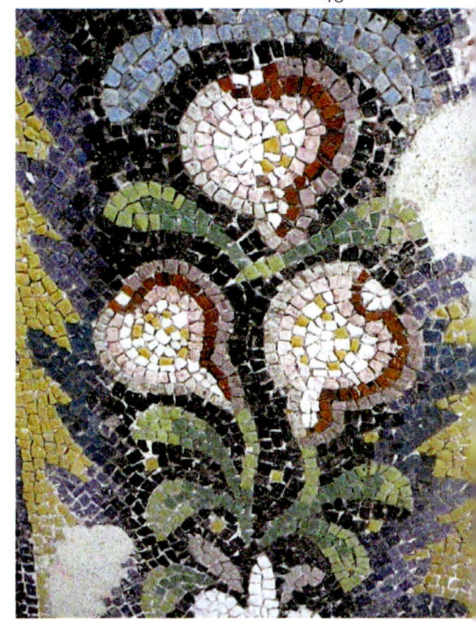

The tesserae in the Rotunda mosaics differ considerably in size and shape. The gold and silver cubes are generally larger than those of coloured glass. The size is often chosen in relation to the particular needs of a given motif. For example, in the architectural zone, large silver pieces with a diameter of 2.5 centimetres are placed in columns to imitate mother-of-pearl. Other tesserae are tiny, measuring merely a few millimetres. The smallest pieces are those of limestone used for the martyr portraits. The skin of faces and hands were set in white, beige and several shades of rose limestone. This extensive use of limestone and marble is a special characteristic of the Rotunda mosaics.

Before the actual setting of the mosaics, the artists needed to do some preliminary preparations. First of all, horizontal and vertical guidelines and sketches (such as those remaining for Christ and the angels) were painted directly on the brickwork. Sometimes the scale had to be adjusted. This was the case for the image of Christ; in its final stage, it was considerably scaled down in relation to the sketch. The next step was to prepare the ground with three layers of mortar of increasing fineness. Some of the iron clamps still visible in the middle zone of the cupola (in the area where the large angels once were dancing) served for securing the mortar to the ground. The final mortar layer was applied to an area no larger than could be set in a single day. It was on this layer that the artists painted the images. In fact, before the motifs were set in mosaic, they were executed as complete wall paintings. The mosaicists would then work on top of these paintings while they were still wet and soft, copying them by inserting the tesserae, one by one in the painted setting bed. For the martyr portraits a different method was used. As noted above, the heads were made separately by specialists in workshops and then set into the bodies of the saints that had been finished *in situ* in the cupola.

The conservative nature of the mosaic technique employed in the Rotunda is quite remarkable. Indeed, the setting technique is closely related to that of Hellenistic mosaic floors from various parts of the eastern Mediterranean of the second and first centuries BC. In floors, especially from Delos and Alexandria, one finds the minute *opus vermiculatum* ("worm work") setting technique, which is characteristic of the martyr portraits. Chequerboard patterns of squares in alternating colours, as seen in the martyrs' complexion, is another Hellenistic device; in floor mosaics it often served for rendering glittering fish scales. Finally, the naturalistic depiction of fruit and flowers in the wreath that encircles the medallion and in the vegetal decorations of the light-openings [43] at the base of the cupola is quite close to similar designs in Hellenistic floors.

The setting technique, the choice of colours and materials and the combination of stone and glass define the stylistic characteristics of the mosaics. The specific mosaic technique is therefore important for evaluating the aesthetic qualities of the mosaics.

Aesthetic Aspects of the Mosaics

Silver and golden mosaics have a special appeal. Depending on the time of day and on how the light falls on the mosaics, the cupola and vaults show various degrees of shimmer and shine. Even in dim light, the gold of the architectural zone is the dominant visual feature. Due to the variant shapes of the tesserae and their irregular, slightly inclined setting, the golden surfaces appear animated with continually shifting motion. All the golden areas have this undefinable, immaterial quality that makes the mosaic ground appear as a fond of light. The conventional ideas of foreground, middle-ground and background are dissolved. The fantastic golden architecture is outlined against this golden luminosity, wherein buildings and human figures carve their proper niches. What may potentially lie behind the figures and objects remains hidden. Where nothing is represented, gold fills the void. Thus the gold also serves to unite the individual motifs.

With its columns and pediments, small pavilions and fine architectural details, where red and green curtains stand out as coloured accents and draw the eye to the imagery, the scenography brings to mind some of the best of Roman wall painting. But whereas the painted structures are rendered in strongly contrasting hues such as red, purple and turquoise, in the mosaics, the forms and colours are transformed into light itself, in a bejewelled golden aesthetic. The buildings seem to emerge from an infinite wellspring of light. By a sophisticated use of perspective, the viewer is invited to enter the holy Jerusalem. To see the mosaics in the proper way, one must imagine oneself to be "up there", having joined the martyrs in the splendid heavenly scenery.

In order to obtain specific colouristic effects, the artists experimented with different ways of setting the mosaic tesserae in the saints' fine attire. Some are dressed in white, others in purple, but within the white and purple there is subtle variation. Kosmas' white *paenula* is interspersed with silver (now for the most part lost), while that of his companion brother Damianos is, in addition to silver, interspersed with tesserae of an olive tone. This gives it a yellowish tint. Turning to the soldiers, the large inset on their cloaks, the *tablion*, is remarkable for being differently coloured in each cloak. Seen from a distance, all *tablia* appear purple. In some soldiers' *tablia* it is possible in daylight to make out the presence of different colours within the purple area. But a close-up view is required to see all the minutiae of these designs. The *tablia* are composed mainly of blue, red and orange tesserae, set in minute chequerboard patterns alternating with parallel vertical lines [44]. Experimenting with colours, the artists must have noticed that red tesserae next to blue tesserae gave the impression of purple when the mosaics were viewed from a distance [18]. The purple colour of these areas is therefore an optical phenomenon. For the angels, a variant form of optical blending is used to give the impression of colourful wings, fluttering in gentle motion.

44. Close-up of Onesiphoros' *tablion* disclosing impressionistic colour setting in red, blue and orange. When seen from a distance the colours blended into purple.

One can compare this blending technique to that used by late nineteenth-century French painters. In their pointillist and divisionist paintings, Georges Seurat and Paul Signac juxta-

44

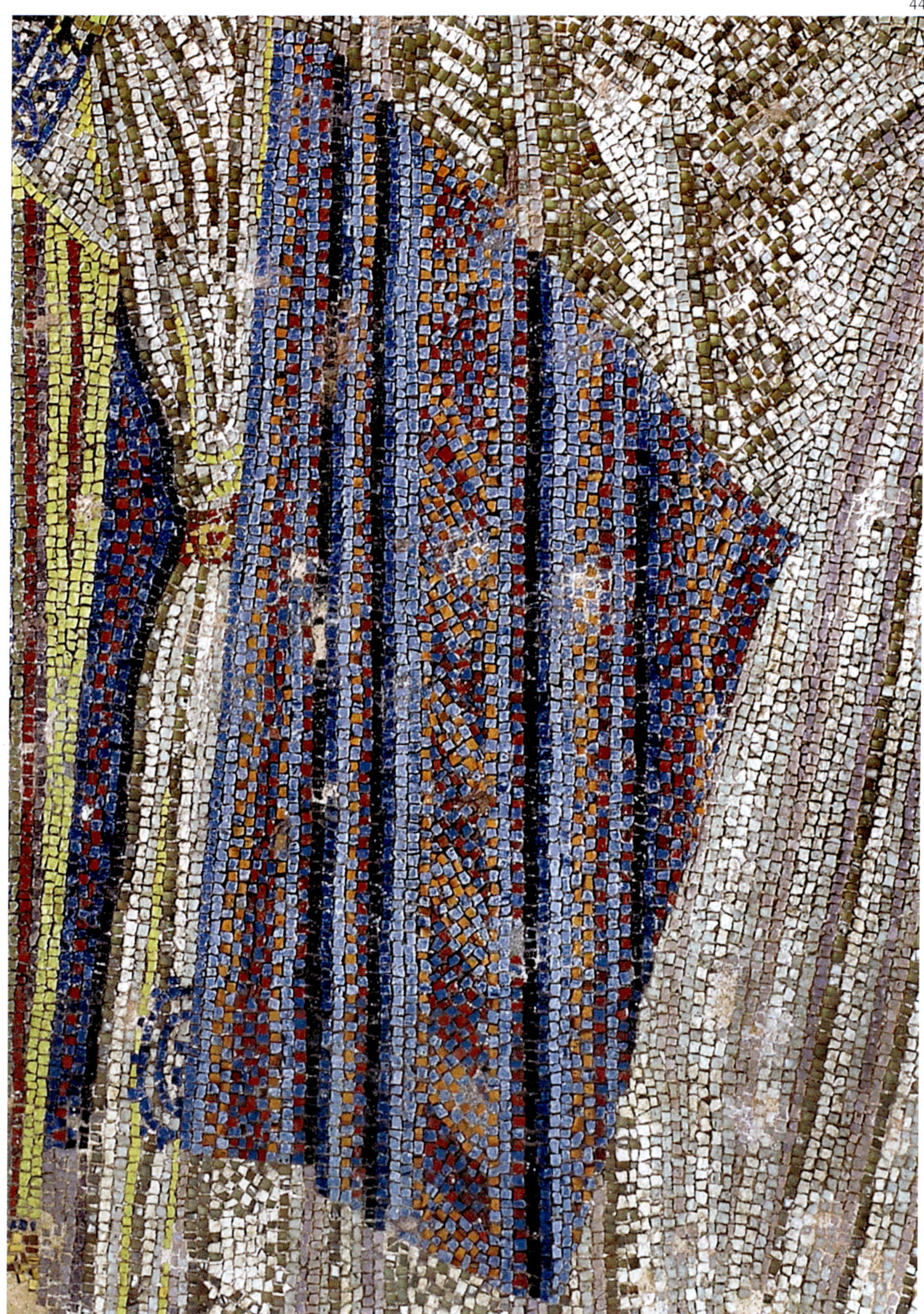

posed small dots of paint which optically blended into other colours when seen from a distance. As can now be experienced from the floor in the Rotunda: the colour achieved by the optical method is more intense, saturated and bright than the purple and violet hues obtained in the conventional manner by setting only violet tesserae. The two methods are juxtaposed in the violet cloaks of the soldier saints Leon (SE) and Eukarpion (W) [45]. In them we clearly see that the purple *tablion* is brighter than the violet colour of the cloak. Moreover, optical blending of red, blue and orange makes the surface shine with a silken sheen. It therefore serves to simulate the very finest textiles. In their work, the artists visualized the aesthetic concept of *poikilia*: diversity, complexity and shifting visual impressions.

Face to face with the martyrs, one can appreciate other colouristic intricacies. A specific characteristic is the choice of colour in the portrait heads. Most of the martyrs have violet to purple eyes, only the three young soldiers Leon, Onesiphoros and Basiliskos have blue eyes. It is noticeable that the hair, which when seen from the floor gives a general impression of light or dark, is not set in ordinary hair colour such as brown or black. While Leon, Onesiphoros and the anonymous soldier have hair in shades ranging from yellow to dark red, the prevalent hair colour is purple to violet, tending towards bluish silver in older martyrs. In antiquity, purple (porphyreos, πορφύρεος) was perceived as a bright and splendid colour, and the word *porphyreos* also meant gleaming.

The artists wanted to make the martyrs appear almost translucent with hair and garments of woven light. By means of light-reflecting tesserae, the mosaicists imbued the holy faces with a lustrous quality that makes them appear illuminated from within. Through the symbolic use of colour, the saints are visualized not in a transient moment of historical reality, but in a timeless existence of ideal beauty.

Colour and light are intimately associated with each other in Byzantine aesthetics of all periods, and in the Rotunda mo-

45. Soldier martyr Eukarpion dressed in purple chlamys.

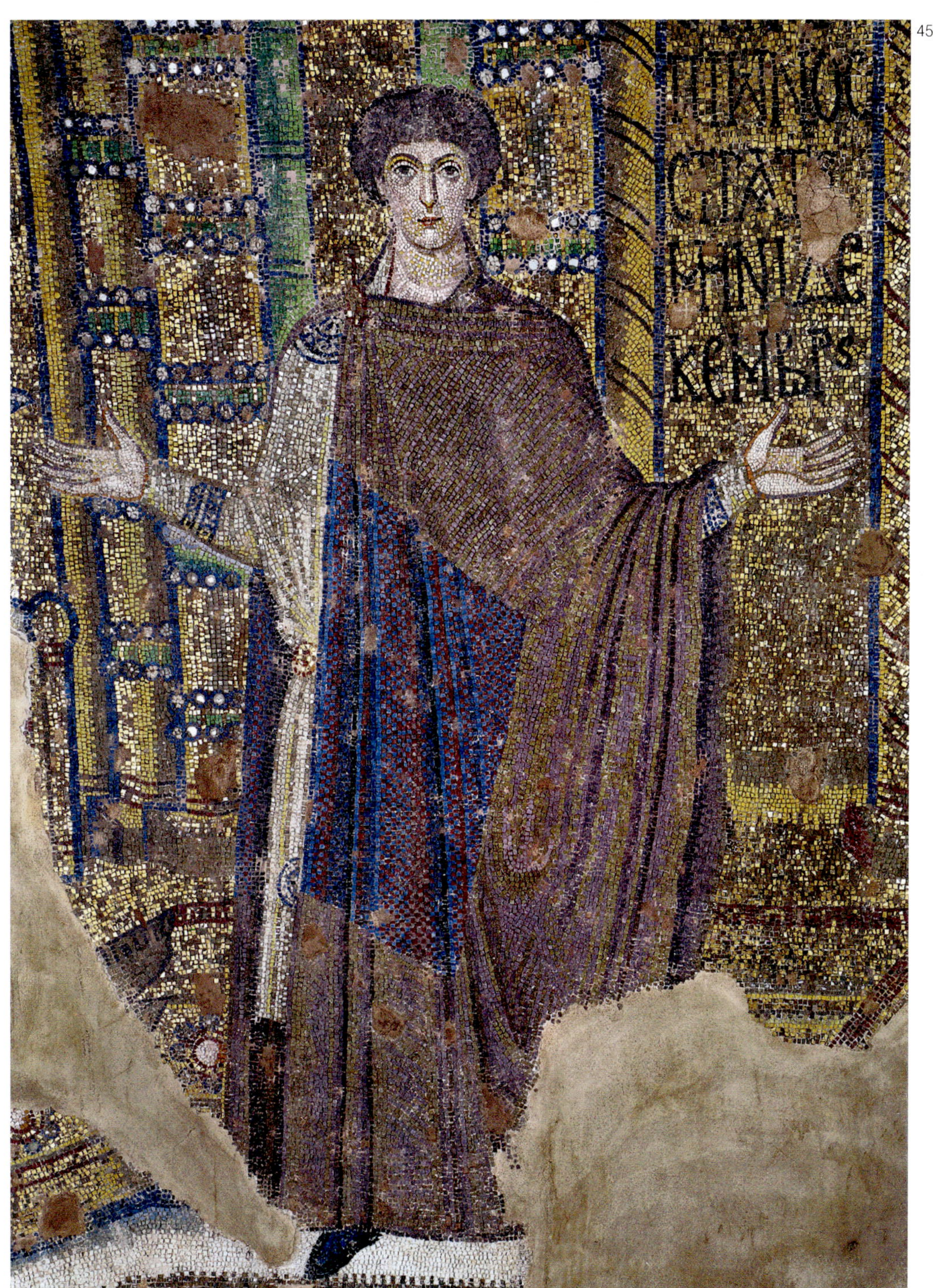

45

saics, divine light is undoubtedly the "leading feature". Using a profusion of gold and silver, the artists created the impression of a divinely lit space. At the top of the cupola, Christ, who was probably dressed in purple, white and gold, emerged from blazing silver light. He was illuminated by a circle of shining stars and the multi-coloured light of the rainbow. The four angels also wore shiny white garments embellished with purple, silver and gold. The architectural zone presented a golden panorama, and the mosaics in the barrel vaults were set in gold and in the entrance vault in silver. The impression of a divinely lit space would have been further enhanced by the light from hundreds of oil lamps, and their reflections in the polished marble revetments on walls and flooring.

CONCLUSION: THE PICTORIAL PROGRAMME

The mosaics in the Rotunda show how a basically antique visual language was adapted by Christianity to serve a new function. Christ in the guise of Helios may allude to the statue of Constantine-Helios that once stood atop the porphyry column in Constantinople. Accompanied by the Phoenix of Roman descent, the floral wreath derives from the Roman triumphal sign of victory and imperial *aeternitas* (eternal power and authority). The angels supporting the cosmic shield with the figure of Christ-Helios are only slightly transformed Victories. The architectural zone reflects late Hellenistic and Roman painted scenography. Finally, the martyrs' portraiture is wholly in the antique tradition; typological parallels to young, mature and old men are found in Mediterranean art, such as floor mosaics and the Fayum portraits. It is obvious that for the decoration of the cupola, Greco-Roman iconographical formulae were refashioned into a new artistic idiom with a Christian meaning: a *reinterpretatio christiana* on a grand and exuberant scale.

The medallion of Christ and the intermediate zone of angels constitute one unified image of the upper spheres of the heavenly world, the spheres that the martyrs, standing in their proper and distinctively framed lower zone, contemplate with wide-open eyes. In sum: the medallion visualizes a theophany of Christ, who is carried by four angels and saluted by a choir of angels, contemplated by the martyrs and by the congregation. The visible manifestation of Christ is immediate, but also timeless and infinite. Fundamentally, then, the mosaics symbolize Christ's continuous and eternal presence in the church and amongst the faithful.

Timeline

ca 305 Building phase I: Galerius constructs the Roman Rotunda.

ca 380/90 Building phase II: Conversion of the Roman Rotunda into a church; most likely by Theodosius the Great. The church is probably dedicated to Christ and the martyrs.

ca 500/550 Building phase III: Following an earthquake in Thessaloniki, the dome is repaired, the ambo is installed (now in Istanbul Archaeological Museum), and the octagonal baptistery west of the entrance is constructed.
The Rotunda becomes the Metropolis of Thessaloniki.

ca 620 Building phase IV: The choir and ambulatory are destroyed in an earthquake; the dome is repaired.

ca 800 The Rotunda is known as the Church of the Asomatoi. Painting of the Ascension added in the apse.

1590/91 The Rotunda is turned into a mosque.
The Rotunda is known as the Church of Saint George.

1667/68 Painted restoration of east mosaic panel (repaired in 1890).

1917 The Rotunda becomes the Museum of Macedonia.

1978 Earthquake followed by substantial restorations.

1988 The Rotunda is one of fifteen Thessalonikan monuments inscribed on UNESCO's World Heritage List.

2015 The scaffolds are removed from the interior of the Rotunda.

Select Bibliography (after 2000)

Architecture, Rotunda, Galerius' Palace:

Athanassiou, F., et al., *The Galerian Complex. A Visual Tour* (Thessaloniki: Hellenic Ministry of Culture. 16th Ephorate, 2013).

Ćurčić, S., *Some Observations and Questions Regarding Early Christian Architecture in Thessaloniki* (Thessaloniki: Ephorate of Byzantine Antiquities of Thessaloniki, 2000).

Duval, N., "Hommage à Ejnar et Ingrid Dyggve; la théorie du palais du Bas-Empire et les fouilles de Thessalonique", *Antiquité Tardive* 11 (2003), 273–300.

Μουτσόπουλος, N.K., *Η Ροτόντα του Αγίου Γεωργίου στη Θεσσαλονίκη. Αρχαιολογική έρευνα και αναστήλωση του μνημείου* (Thessaloniki: Δέσποινα Κυριακίδη 2012).

Στεφανίδου-Τιβερίου, Θ., "Το ανακτορικό συγκρότημα του Γαλερίου στη Θεσσαλονίκη. Σχεδιασμός και χρονολόγηση", *Egnatia* 10 (2006), 163–188.

Stefanidou-Tiberiou, Th., "Die Palastanlage des Galerius in Thessaloniki. Planung und Datierung", in *Diocletian, Tetrarchy and Diocletian's Palace on the 1700th Anniversary of Existence* (Split 2009), 389–409.

Torp, H., "L'entrée septentrionale du palais impérial de Thessalonique: L'arc de Triomphe et le *vestibulum* d'après les fouilles d'Ejnar Dyggve en 1939", *Antiquité Tardive* 11 (2003), 239–272.

Mosaics:

Bakirtzis, Ch. – E. Kourkoutidou-Nikolaïdou – Ch. Mavropoulou-Tsioumi, *Mosaics of Thessaloniki, 4th–14th Century* (Athens: Kapon Editions, 2012), 48–127.

Bakirtzis, Ch. – P. Mastora, "Are the Mosaics in the Rotunda in Thessaloniki Linked to its Conversion to a Christian Church?", in *Niš and Byzantium* IX: Ninth Symposium, June 2010 (Niš 2011), 33–45.

Eastmond, A. – M. Hatzaki, eds., *The Mosaics of Thessaloniki Revisited* (Athens: Kapon Editions, in press).

Fourlas, B., *Die Mosaiken der Acheiropoietos-Basilika in Thessaloniki* (Berlin: de Gruyter, 2012), 177–195.

Hatzaki, M., "Peacocks, Rainbows and Handsome Men: Perceiving Physical Beauty in the Early Byzantine Mosaics of Thessaloniki", in A. Eastmond – M. Hatzaki, eds., *The Mosaics of Thessaloniki Revisited* (Athens: Kapon Editions, in press).

Kiilerich, B., "Picturing Ideal Beauty: The Saints in the Rotunda at Thessaloniki", *Antiquité Tardive* 15 (2007), 321–336.

Kiilerich, B., "Optical Colour Blending in the Rotunda Mosaics", *Musiva & Sectilia* 8 (2011) [2014], 63–92.

Kiilerich, B., *Visual Dynamics: Reflections on Late Antique Images* (Bergen 2015), 123–131. (https://uib.academia.edu/BenteKiilerich/Books)

Kiilerich, B. "Colour, Light and Luminosity in the Rotunda Mosaics", in A. Eastmond – M. Hatzaki, eds., *The Mosaics of Thessaloniki Revisited* (Athens: Kapon Editions, in press).

Mastora., P., "Ο ψηφιδωτός διάκοσμος στις φωτιστικές θυρίδες της Ροτόντας Θεσσαλονίκης", *Archaeologike Ephemeris* 149 (2010), 83–107.

Mentzos, A., "Reflections on the Interpretation and Dating of the Rotunda of Thessaloniki", *Egnatia* 6 (2001–2002), 57–82.

Nasrallah, L., "Empire and Apocalypse in Thessaloniki: Interpreting the Early Christian Rotunda", *Journal of Early Christian Studies* 13 (2005), 465–508.

Torp, H., "Un décor de voûte controversé: l'ornementation 'sassanide' d'une mosaïque de la Rotonde de Saint-Georges à Thessalonique", *Acta ad archaeologiam et artium historiam pertinentia*, n.s. 15 (2001), 295–317.

Torp, H., "Dogmatic Themes in the Mosaics of the Rotunda at Thessaloniki", *Arte medievale*, n.s. I, 1 (2002), 11–34.

Torp, H., "Les mosaïques de la Rotonde de Thessalonique: l'arrière-fond conceptuel des images d'architecture", *Cahiers archéologiques* 50 (2002), 3–20.

Torp, H., "La iconizzazione musiva dell'enunciato politico-religioso di un editto imperiale", in *Medioevo: immagine e racconto*, ed. A.C. Quintavalle (Milano: Electa, 2003), 77–86.

Torp, H., "An Interpretation of the Early Byzantine Martyr Inscriptions in the Rotunda at Thessaloniki", *Acta ad archaeologiam et artium historiam pertinentia*, n.s. 10, XXIV (2011), 11–43.

Torp, H., "La technique des mosaïques de la Rotonde de Thessalonique", *Arte medievale* IV. ser., anno IV (2014), 267–282.

Torp, H., "Considerations on the Chronology of the Rotunda Mosaics", in A. Eastmond – M. Hatzaki, eds., *The Mosaics of Thessaloniki Revisited* (Athens: Kapon Editions, in press).

Torp, H., *La Rotonde palatiale à Thessalonique* (forthcoming).

PHOTO CREDITS

Kapon Editions: 1, 3, 4, 7, 14, 16, 23, 31, 32.

B. Kiilerich: 10, 25, 28, 33 (M. Brochmann, based on reconstruction by H. Torp), 34–36 (F. Kirk and M. Brochmann, based on reconstruction by H. Torp), 37 (drawing S. Sass), 42, 43.

BOOKS

Ch. Bakirtzis – E. Kourkoutidou-Nikolaïdou – Ch. Mavropoulou-Tsioumi, *Mosaics of Thessaloniki, 4th–14th Century*, Athens 2012, Kapon Editions. Figs: 2 (drawing W.S. George, BRF 01.01.07.197), 8, 9, 11–13,15, 17, 18–22, 24, 26–27, 29, 30, 44.

G. Ch. Chourmouziadis, *The Gold of the World,* Athens 1997, Kapon Editions. Fig.: 39.

E. Kourkoutidou-Nikolaïdou – A. Tourta, *Wandering in Byzantine Thessaloniki,* Athens 1997, Kapon Editions. Figs: 5, 6, 38, 40, 41, 45.

ARTISTIC DESIGNER: RACHEL MISDRACHI-KAPON

ARTISTIC ADVISOR: MOSES KAPON

COPY EDITOR: DIANA ZAFEIROPOULOU

DTP: ELENI VALMA, MINA MANTA, DEMETRA POULAKI

PROCESSING OF ILLUSTRATIONS: MICHALIS TZANNETAKIS

PRINTING: ELIKON LTD

BINDING: I. BOUNDAS - P. VASILIADIS Co